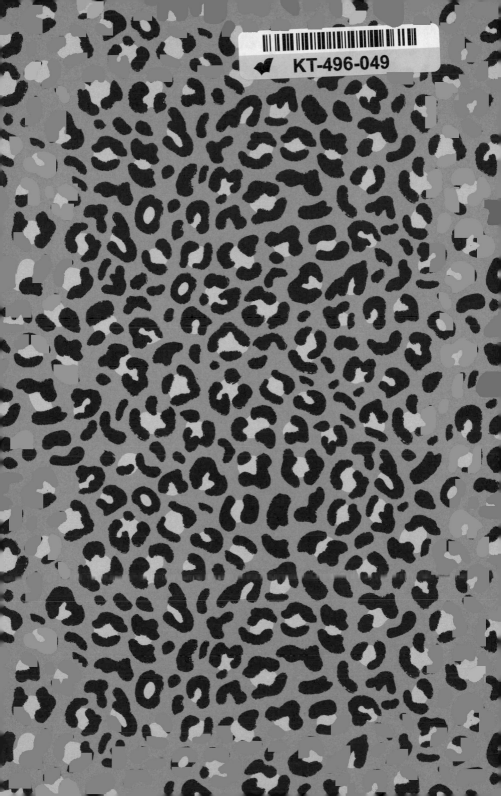

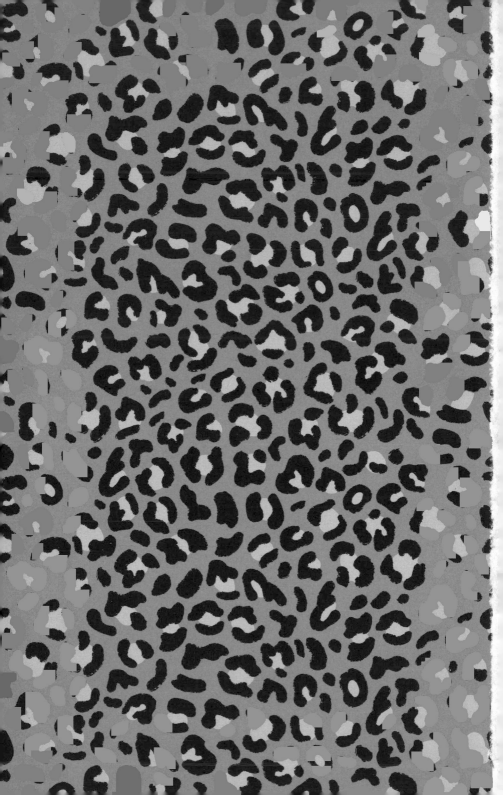

WOMEN DON'T OWE YOU PRETTY

An Hachette UK Company
www.hachette.co.uk

First published in Great Britain in 2020
by Cassell, an imprint of
Octopus Publishing Group Ltd
Carmelite House
50 Victoria Embankment
London EC4Y 0DZ
www.octopusbooks.co.uk

ISBN 978-1-78840-211-8

A CIP catalogue record for this book is available
from the British Library.

Printed and bound in Italy.

018

Cover photography by Chloe Sheppard

Senior commissioning editor: Romilly Morgan
Senior editor: Pauline Bache
Senior designer: Jaz Bahra
Typography and illustrations: Florence Given
Copyeditor: Jo Smith
Diversity reader: Philippa Willitts
Typesetter: Jeremy Tilston at The Oak Studio
Senior production manager: Peter Hunt

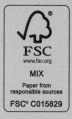

FSC
www.fsc.org
MIX
Paper from
responsible sources
FSC® C015829

WOMEN DON'T OWE YOU PRETTY

FLORENCE GIVEN

FLORENCE GIVEN (SHE / HER) is a UK-based artist and writer. In 2019, Florence was named *Cosmopolitan*'s Influencer of the Year. She has been interviewed on BBC Breakfast to discuss the stigma around being single and NBC News to discuss the campaign she led against fatphobic show *Insatiable*. She has also worked alongside Always on their #EndPeriodPoverty campaign and her post received more than 200k likes, with each like resulting in a free sanitary product for those in need.

 @florencegiven

CONTENTS

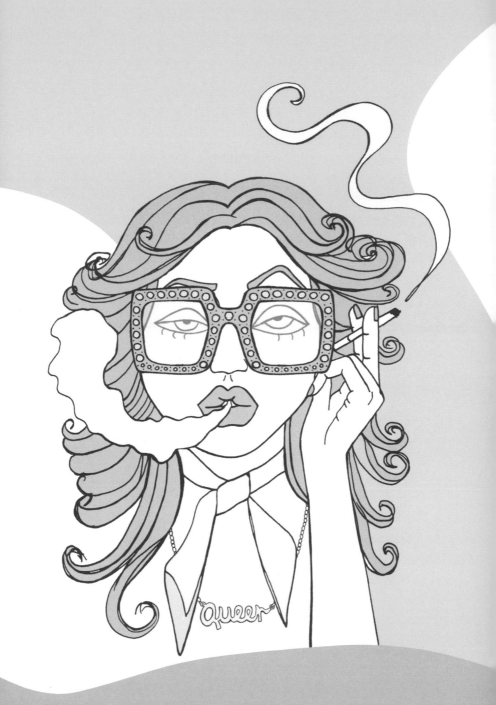

AN INTRODUCTION

"You don't owe prettiness to anyone. Not to your boyfriend/
spouse/partner, not to your co-workers, especially not to
random men on the street. You don't owe it to your mother, you
don't owe it to your children, you don't owe it to civilization in
general. Prettiness is not a rent you pay for occupying a space
marked 'female'." – Erin McKean

This quote changed my life and inspired the title of this book.

Throughout feminist history, women have expanded on the concept
of prettiness as a currency from their different standpoints, and there are
a lot of variations on this idea out there. For example, Naomi Wolf's book
The Beauty Myth unpacks in-depth how our beauty standards are linked
to capitalism; Chidera Eggerue touches on prettiness in her book *What a
Time to Be Alone* and in her #SaggyBoobsMatter movement to promote a
message of anti-perfection; and trans activist Janet Mock speaks on how
she felt she gained pretty privilege as she began her transition. This book
– *Women Don't Owe You Pretty* – is my interpretation.

This phrase sent me on a journey of unpacking my identity, forcing
me to properly examine myself for the first time and ask why the hell
I was carrying out these invasive, expensive, time-consuming and at
times *painful* beauty rituals. I realized how much of my self-worth was
determined by whether or not I appeared desirable to men, and whether
that prettiness would be enough to encourage them to treat me with
respect. But most of the time the attention that my "prettiness" garnered
meant that men viewed me as an object, and men don't respect objects.
After all, objects are something we view to be used without reciprocity

– it's a one-sided relationship. It's why they didn't handle my rejection well and called me names like "frigid", because objects aren't supposed to be empowered. They're objects. Acknowledging this was both uncomfortable and liberating – exactly what growth is supposed to feel like.

This phrase also forced me to examine the kinds of standards against which someone's "prettiness" is measured, and what "pretty" constitutes. Our collective idea of what makes someone pretty in society is based on their proximity to whiteness, thinness, being non-disabled and being cisgender. This helped me to see how my own prettiness has enabled me opportunities, opportunities that women who fall outside of what society deems as pretty have to work harder for. Whether I thought I was attractive or not, for the first time I had to acknowledge the objective fact that I sit high on society's scale of desirability, by being slim, non-disabled and white. As women we don't want to admit that we have "pretty privilege" because we have been taught that we should be unaware of our beauty, and to respond to compliments with self-deprecation and remarks such as "No I'm not, look at my...[points to 'flaws']!" In order to acknowledge that we have this privilege, we must first call ourselves *pretty*. Which, due to insecurity, is near impossible for most women. This is how our desirability privilege is silently maintained, and how as a society we continue to go about de-politicizing our dating preferences as if they aren't problematic and heavily loaded with racist, fatphobic and sexist bias.

There's a discussion about whether desirability really is a privilege, since its benefits are rooted in the objectification of our bodies, not respecting them. My prettiness is both the thing that allows people to treat me better, and also the thing that has led to the most traumatic experiences of my life. Men don't look at pretty women on the street and think "She's pretty, so I won't sexually harass her or follow her home." It's the opposite. I walk about life with constant vigilance – anxious for the next man to stick his head out his car window and shout something at me, spike the drink that my "prettiness" encouraged him to buy for me – and stop in a shop before I go home to check I'm not being followed. Keys between my fingers, heart racing, checking over my shoulder, strategizing my safest route home even if it means spending money on a taxi – this is what navigating public spaces looks like for a lot of women. I can't tell you the amount of times I have contemplated shaving my head to rid me of male attention and sexual harassment almost entirely overnight. But I realized that to do so would imply that it's my responsibility to prevent this harassment, and that women who choose a "feminine" appearance are "asking for it".

I was taught how to count calories, have boundaries with and say "no" to food as a young girl, before I learned about the importance of having boundaries and saying "no" to other people. What do you think that taught me about being a woman in this world? I learned that it was more important for me to be an object of desire, than it was to have my own needs met and be respected as a person. These harmful belief systems and low self-esteem landed me in abusive relationships as my boundaries were non-existent and I didn't believe I deserved better. I was just happy that someone *wanted me*.

I often wonder what my life would look like if I had learned that my body belongs to me, and me alone, first; that the way my body looks and its purpose is not to please others. I wonder what my life would look like if I had understood that I do not owe anybody "nice", "perfect", "petite" or "pretty"; that the best version of myself is not the one that is broken down in order to fit into the room afforded for women in a man's world, but is the version that stays whole in spite of other people's reactions – whether there is space for me or not.

Instead, I killed, squashed and minimized parts of who I really was in favour of the validation I craved, living to please everyone but myself – and I don't want you to feel as though you have to do the same. This is the book I wish I could have whacked myself over the head with before the world's toxicity permeated its way into my life.

Here's what a conversation between my younger self and older self would have sounded like.

Older Floss: Floss – why are you stuffing your bra and skipping breakfast?

Younger Floss: Because that's what boys like! Skinny girls with big tits.

OF: Okay Floss, can I have a word?

YF: Yeah, what's the problem?

OF: I understand why you feel the way you do, but...

YF: Yeah? All the popular girls are doing it.

OF: Well, what you do with your body is your choice and your choice only. But I think it's really important for you to understand the real reason behind your choices. Because what you're doing to yourself is actually very unhealthy. Can you tell me why you're skipping meals? What's your reason behind this?

YF: Because "nothing tastes as good as skinny feels"! I'm not doing it for men. I just like the way it looks.

OF: Jesus. Okay. First of all, I know you're in 2013 right now, but it's 2020 where I am and Kate Moss herself has since publicly regretted ever saying that. Your weight does not define you and it is not a measure of your beauty, that concept is now OBSOLETE. Second of all, the reason you want to do this to yourself may not be consciously motivated by wanting to attract men, but our collective idea as a society of what is "pretty" and "desirable" is informed entirely by racism, sexism, fatphobia, disablism, transphobia and male desire. So even though you're doing it "because you want to", the reason you think big boobs and skinniness is beautiful is because it's what men want, and we consume their ideas of beauty through the media, films and television. Do you notice how boys just show up to school in their uniform, with scruffy hair and sleep in their eyes?

YF: But it's just different for bo... Oh. I see. Yeah I guess that's not fair, is it?

OF: No, it isn't. While the boys get to wake up ten minutes before school starts, put on their uniform and scoff down their breakfast, you spend an entire morning looking in the mirror making yourself up in a way that you hope those same boys would desire you, skipping your breakfast in an attempt to be a slim, pretty object of their affection. You must be exhausted. Have you ever thought about what you could do with that extra time? Have you ever wondered what your life might look like if you just showed up, as you are?

YF: Wow, I hadn't thought of it like that. I guess it would be easier if I could just roll out of bed and turn up...but still, all the popular girls do it and I want to be popular! Life is easier when I make myself look pretty! It's normal – all the girls in the magazines and movies who get the guy are the prettiest. All the men want to date them!

OF: And why do you feel so strongly that men need to desire you?

YF: Doesn't every woman feel that way? I thought that's just the way the world works...women make themselves pretty so men can desire them.

OF: So, you believe a woman's worth is tied up in her ability to be pretty?

YF: I never thought about it like that. I guess, maybe I do...

OF: So, if you feel that way, and you believe that your worth as a woman is tied up in your beauty, how do you feel about women who aren't pretty? Do you look down on them? Do you think they're worthless?

YF: I don't think I do. But perhaps...

OF: Do you feel you make yourself look this way because you like it, or are you performing femininity out of routine so you can be treated better by other people? The same way you know deep down that you yourself are nicer to women who perform femininity?

YF: OH MY GOD STOP ATTACKING ME!

OF: It wasn't an attack, Floss. These questions are acting as a mirror, and they're forcing you to see the ugly parts of your internalized hatred towards other women and femininity. Reflect on it, and answer my question!

YF: Well, if I don't go to school with make-up and my hair looking nice people always mention it, they say I look tired. People treat me way better and acknowledge me when I look pretty, so I figured I'd conform! I get what you're saying. It's not fair and men get to just show up as they are blah blah blah. But surely if I look more pretty and make myself up in the image of what men want, then they will choose me!

OF: Why do you feel the need to be chosen by men? Why can't you just go to school – to learn?

YF: I – don't actually know. Again, it's what I've always been told

I should want – a man, that is. I guess I never thought to ask myself why I want to be "chosen by men", or where that came from.

OF: So, ask yourself now!

YF: Because it's what everyone else is doing? I saw it in movies? All girls try to look good for men! I don't know, that's just the way it is!

OF: Well Floss, you're not wrong. A man is more likely to choose you if you perform femininity and make yourself up in the image of their desire...

YF: This is what I'm trying to say!

OF: ...but not in the way you want men to choose you.

YF: Oh.

OF: If you have to perform a level of "prettiness" in order to be chosen by someone, they are choosing you based on your objective beauty. I get that you crave to be chosen by someone based on more than how you look. You want to be chosen for your entire self. Darling, as long as you spend your years chasing male validation, you will exhaust yourself all the way to your grave. Because male validation is a bottomless pit. It won't ever see you how you deserve to be seen. Stop chasing it. Stop trying to attract it. Stop trying to mould yourself into a palatable Floss. It will consume you and spit you back out once it's done using you. Your main goal in life is not to be "chosen" by a man anyway. It's all a big lie. You don't actually need men for anything. Or at the very least, not in the capacity you've been made to think you do.

YF: WAIT, WHAT?! I thought we needed men for like...everything?!

OF: Not true.

YF: What about money? I've always thought I'd marry a rich man...

OF: If that's what you want to do, that's fine. But also, go make your own money first. You are a rich man.

YF: Fine – what about having kids?

OF: Do you even want kids? Or do you feel a pressure to have them because, as well as her ability to be beautiful, a woman's worth in this society has also been based on her ability to reproduce? You are not a failure if you do not have children...

YF: Jesus – not have children? I'll get back to you on that one. What about for sex, and love? We need men for sex!

OF: Buy a vibrator. Also, contrary to the messaging of mainstream media that you have been consuming your entire life, men aren't the only option for a potential romantic partner! Have you ever considered that you might be attracted to other genders?

YF: Well shit.

OF: What?!

YF: I've always wanted to date women and people of other genders, but I've been afraid to express this because I'm attracted to men too, and figured my feelings for other people were invalid...

OF: You see! We are taught in so many ways that we need to rely on men to be happy. But you don't. And by the way hun, you're queer as hell.

YF: So, what you're saying is that I only require men to be in my life in a capacity that adds to my already amazing existence?

OF: YES...

YF: I don't have to compromise myself because...I'm enough on my own?

OF: YES! Encouraging women to spend hours focusing on their prettiness and desirability for men, instead of directing that energy towards themselves, is a very intentional method to make sure that men keep making all the money, having all the fun and having lots of sex, while women are expected to compete for their attention and are shamed for doing the exact same things men do.

YF: Why would women be shamed for doing the same things as men? That doesn't seem fair.

OF: You're right, it isn't. But it happens. Because when women choose to behave outside of our appointed, prescribed gender roles, it unravels centuries of oppressive structures and some people can't handle their reality being challenged. In the name of preserving this "tradition" they use the tool of shame to keep us in our place. An example is how women are called "bitches" for being assertive, setting firm boundaries or standing up for themselves. Most of the time, it's not even men who call women bitches. When we turn against each other, it's patriarchy's very sneaky way of continuing our oppression – because it gets other women to do its dirty work, so it doesn't look guilty of being the reason we are taught to compete with and hate each other in the first place.

YF: Wait, so you're saying that sexism and double standards are just a big trick to stop us focusing on our careers, making our own money, having sex and enjoying our lives, instead encouraging us to fight with each other and believe that we need men and that we can't live without them?

OF: Pretty much.

YF: Surely some women can have it all – right?

OF: Some women might appear to have it all – living their best lives with thriving careers, lots of sex, they may have children too – but this comes at a price. We will not be treated in the same way men are for doing this. People will laugh at you, shame you, you will be called "selfish" for trying to achieve the same lifestyle as a man, and often you'll find that you are paid less for doing the same job a man does. This is actually going to happen to you by the way, quite a few times. Ready yourself.

YF: But what's the point in "being myself" if that version of me is going to be treated poorly and criticized? Why don't I just carry on the way I am, performing femininity for men, and living in the roles supplied to me, so the world continues to reward me with unearned benefits?

OF: Points well made. I hear your confusion, and that's a very important and valid question. Performing femininity and prettiness for a lot of women is survival. You're right. Why would you take the route of "being yourself" when you know that there's a much easier, well-travelled route. One where you are treated better, and all you have to do is grab a make-up brush and a razor!

YF: That's what I mean!

OF: Right! You are seen when you look pretty. Men like it when you shrink yourself down, because this dynamic confirms their masculinity.

YF: You mean that when I make myself smaller around a man and "stay in my lane" it's so he can perform his masculinity and not feel threatened by my confidence?

OF: You got it.

YF: Yeah, that feels like...not my problem? Why should I shrink myself for someone else's comfort?

OF: Exactly, it's not your problem. A lot of straight men don't actually know who they are if they aren't able to "provide" for women. You might find yourself subconsciously doing all kinds of ridiculous things to fluff their egos. For example, pretending you don't know a lot about a subject, just so he can explain it to you. Society rewards women who don't have to be told to stay in their lane. It loves women who just readily accept their gender roles and conform, the ones who don't challenge its regime. Doing little things to please men will afford you a lot of advantages.

However, as femininity is associated with "weakness", it can also be the thing that people mistreat us for. You need to look no further than a man's reaction to someone who just told him he's "acting like a girl" to see how true this is. If one of the worst things you can call a man is "a girl" – what kind of message is that sending to girls?

YF: Wow. I guess that explains why I pride myself so much on the parts of my identity that make me "not like the other girls".

OF: Exactly, the "other girls" are all of us. Cut that shit out! This is called internalized misogyny, you are to trying to distance yourself from femininity as much as possible, to win over the attention of men. Women are often not taken seriously because of their femininity. Our higher-pitched voices are mocked to the point that media-trained women are taught to speak lower. You'll be called a "slut" for having casual sex with men, but a "prude" when you reject them. Our cleavage and curves are used to sell products in advertisements for companies run by rich men, but we're told to cover ourselves up when breastfeeding our children, and...

YF: Okay I think I get it. What you're saying is that either way, no matter what I do as a woman – I can't win? There's always going to be compromise?

OF: Yes.

YF: That sucks.

OF: Not if you change your perspective.

YF: How do you mean?

OF: Well, if you're going to be punished either way – tell me. What option does that leave you with?

YF: To do whatever the fuck I want?

OF: Exactly.

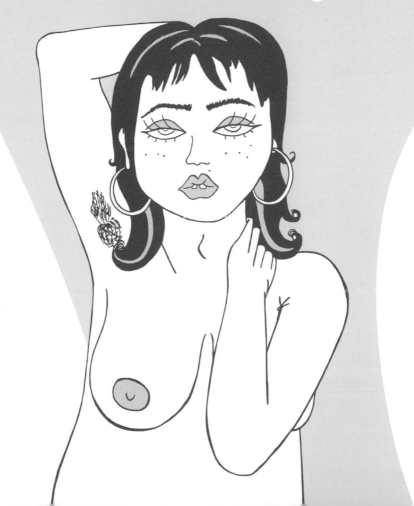

CHAPTER 1

FEMINISM IS GOING TO RUIN YOUR LIFE
(IN THE BEST WAY POSSIBLE)

"A comfort zone is a beautiful place, but nothing ever grows there" – Unknown

My journey into feminism was exhausting.

I lost friends, cried in nightclub toilets because the normalization of groping repulsed me to my core, *screamed* in the faces of men who cat-called me, and fell out with my parents on multiple occasions.

Very on-brand for me.

Very dramatic.

But I had to do this in order to grow. I had to (and still do, regularly) go through a period of sitting in toxic bullshit, abandoning old versions of myself, shedding skins and experiencing this uncomfortable transition to be the person I am today – feeling confident enough in myself and my voice to write this book, speak my mind and vocalize my experiences.

Growth can feel isolating. Everything you thought you knew about yourself and the world shifts right before your eyes. You'll start to notice unhealthy and toxic qualities in your friends, as well as yourself. You'll stop enjoying your once-favourite movies when you realize they portray women as nothing more than a feast for male eyes and desires. The lyrics to your favourite Rolling Stones song start to ring a little problematic, and you'll be disgusted to discover that sexism, racism, ableism and transphobia exist in almost every environment, including the depths of your own subconscious mind. A shift in perspective has the power to flip the world as you know it upside down. But wouldn't you rather see the world clearly, than walk through life oblivious to all that you are complicit in and enabling?

Don't be a passenger in your own life.

Having your world turned upside down and experiencing temporary discomfort is minor in comparison to the suffering you would have endured *and* inflicted onto others over the course of your life if you left these things unchecked. *Temporary discomfort is an investment in your future self.* Accept a small and uncomfortable transition now, for a lifetime of growth and self-development.

Feminism and self-discovery will uproot your entire life, but it's going to be worth it. I promise.

YOU WON'T BE ABLE TO ENJOY THINGS ANYMORE

Enter feminism, the world of hating everything.

Just kidding! *Kind of.*

But baby once those goggles are off there's no going back. You're going to see the misogyny, racism and double standards in absolutely *everything*:

- One minute "chick flicks" are your favourite movies, the next they're the stereotype-perpetuating garbage that you blame for making you crave male validation.
- Past sexual experiences that left you feeling uncomfortable

might now actually be reframed as assault or rape, as you learn to understand more clearly the definition of consent.

- Yes, you'll find yourself enraged over the slightest things. Right down to how much space men take up on public transport with their legs, and how you so instinctively cross yours.
- Yes, you might realize how your own behaviour changes when you interact with men, and how there's an innate urge for you to be polite, desirable and palatable.
- And yes, your eyes are going to open up to the fuckery in our society and your *own* behaviour that was so normalized. You might feel repulsed at yourself for never spotting it in the first place.

But guilt is an unproductive emotion. Feeling guilty for past mistakes and behaviours does nothing for you or the people you harmed, unless it is accompanied by changed behaviour. What matters is that you're aware now, you're waking up, and the actions you take moving forwards are how you stop perpetuating further harm.

YOU WILL LOSE FRIENDS

With growth comes discomfort, this is inevitable. You have to be willing to outgrow your peers, your friends, and even your family, if you're going to live a fulfilled life on your own terms, break cycles and lead a new path. Hopefully, they'll grow with you or support you through your journey. But worrying about what others think when you're growing isn't your priority. Right now, just focus on *growing*.

This is probably the toughest thing you will face as you become more socially, politically and *self* aware. As you outgrow the people in your life and embark on your journey of self-development, you'll see sides of them that you never did before. You might even feel guilty for outgrowing them and believe them when they tell you that you've "taken it too far" or that you're being "too sensitive". But remember that anyone who tells you you're "too" *anything* is using the word because they are threatened by your capacity to grow, evolve and express your emotions. They want you to stay down there, with them – emotionally and morally stunted. You are a mirror reflecting back to them the parts of themselves that they know they're lacking. While this explains their behaviour, it does not excuse it.

People who are emotionally secure and have a strong sense of self won't feel intimidated by your need to express the emotional responses you feel. Those who do are lacking, and you are abundant. Never apologize for this. Being empathic and able to truly *feel* so intensely is a gift, a talent, and something that people strive for.

You do not have to shrink yourself down to make others feel better about themselves.

Stop surrounding yourself with people who make you question your worth, and fill your life instead with people who choose to *remind* you of it – while simultaneously holding you accountable when you mess up. *Both these things are acts of love.*

If I listened to every person who told me I've "taken my feminism too far" or believed every person who told me "not everything's about race/gender/sexuality", I'd still be stuck in my old ways of ignorance and stagnancy, which is *exactly* the type of person the racist patriarchy relies on to keep these systems of oppression alive and thriving. Don't leave conversations about politics to "the grown-ups". *That's what the grown-ups want.* Patriarchy hates progressive conversations and disruptive people because it's a parasite that feeds on *silence and fear* – just as rape culture relies on the silencing of its victims. This is why the #MeToo movement founded by Tarana Burke was so instrumental in raising awareness and challenging the normalization of sexual assault. When people shut you down for "speaking up", it's because they want the status quo to be maintained. It's a tactic as old as time. Stay headstrong. Keep going.

Most people don't want to acknowledge that everything they know is a falsehood. *Who would?* The whole *point* of evolving is that it's an uncomfortable (but necessary) transition. Of course we're going to be reluctant to believe narratives that challenge our whole identity. It means realizing that we have been acting out of ignorance and through our subconscious minds our whole lives. Acknowledging this truth *is* uncomfortable. Knowing you have been unintentionally causing harm and benefitting from unfair systems *is* uncomfortable. But think about how uncomfortable it must be existing on the flip side of that privilege.

Imagine your identity as a woven piece of fabric – from birth your entire identity has been worked into the piece of fabric and makes you who you are today. Threads upon threads make up the unique person you are, just like your DNA. Who you were told to be, who you were told to trust, how you were taught to give and receive love and how you respond to certain situations, all of these factors make up *your* reality as you know it. Now imagine someone coming along and saying something that challenges and unravels the threads of your identity, and how that might make you feel. This is where people can become defensive. Rewiring our toxic and self-destructive patterns isn't supposed to be comfortable, but the more open-minded and aware you are to the fact that we all perceive and live *different realities*, because our fabrics have been woven differently, the easier it becomes to grow, empathize, evolve (and reweave your fabric) with ease and self-awareness.

WORRYING ABOUT WHAT OTHERS THINK WHEN YOU'RE GROWING ISN'T YOUR PRIORITY.

JUST GROW.

STOP JUDGING OTHERS SO HARSHLY FOR THINGS YOU RECENTLY STOPPED DOING YOURSELF

I want to make it clear that people who are at the receiving end of abuse, whether directly from an individual person or by a system of oppression such as racism, don't owe anyone their forgiveness. Rape survivors don't owe their rapist "second chances" because "people make mistakes". People of colour do not owe white people forgiveness. Women do not owe men forgiveness. It's up to them. No one owes their abuser/oppressor *shit*.

I'm talking here about unintentional slip-ups that we ourselves make. Sometimes on our journey of self-development, to cope with the realization that we have perpetuated toxic behaviours and tendencies, we find ourselves taking it out on other people to assuage the guilt we feel about our newly discovered shortcomings. For example, it's only over recent years that I've come to learn how loaded the term "bitch" is when used as an insult. Once I realized how often I'd used this to describe women (who were actually just assertive, and reminded me of my *own* lack of boundaries and *my* inability to say "no"), I'd jump down the throat of anyone around me who used the term "bitch", instead of just informing them the way that I was once informed.

Everyone should be held accountable for their actions, but we still need to extend the same forgiveness and room to grow that was afforded to us when we were still learning. Which, by the way, we still are. Every one of us – every day. We are never done learning. When you decide to stop supporting someone for making a mistake or calling them out to make yourself feel better, it isn't an act of holding someone accountable, it's an act of self-righteousness. It's also ineffective and counter-productive, because no one learns anything and the problem doesn't actually get solved. It just makes *you* feel better about yourself and your own shortcomings.

It's important to acknowledge red flags and abusive behaviours before they become a bigger problem, but people make mistakes. Do you have a friend who's really bad at communicating? Tell them. Your mum making outdated comments about women's bodies, your racist grandma, your friends shaming other women for casual sex, your boyfriend insisting on doing all the "man things" and making jokes about women in the kitchen (just dump him), white girls wearing cornrows, calling them "boxer braids" and singing *that* word in rap songs, your feminist BFF who "doesn't agree" with sex-workers – call them out. Inform them. Their bullshit is their problem, not yours. *They* are the ones who should feel the pressure and guilt to change, not you.

If you have the capacity, you can explain *why* as white people we can't say *that* word (yes, even though Kanye sings it), *how* jokes about "women in the kitchen" perpetuate sexism. Explain to your mum the standards women's bodies are held to in comparison with men's, how we are expected to show up a certain way in this world, and who are we to blame people for conforming under systems of oppression?

Remind your grandma that this isn't the 1960s and you can't say shit like that anymore. In fact, that shit was never okay. Tell your BFF that sex workers are *not* the enemy of progress, that they are in fact exploiting the system built to oppress them, and that this alone is iconic as fuck.

It's a different story when someone is repetitively causing harm. Some people just don't want to change. But you can still be a no bullshit taking zero-tolerance person when it comes to sexist, racist, transphobic, disablist, homophobic bullshit, while also allowing room for people to prove to you that they can grow, learn from mistakes and bounce back with changed behaviour – *just like you did.*

It's difficult when someone you love is saying something wrong and you don't want to correct them in case you come off as too "political" or "sensitive". But these are *exactly* the discussions you need to be having to change the world.

Some people go their entire lives without even questioning their identity, attempting to deconstruct patterns or end cycles of inherited trauma, because they're too focused on *surviving*. It's easier to live by the narrative that has been supplied since birth because they don't have time to think about evolving. Having time to unpack and evaluate is in itself a privilege! Having access to the internet and so many diverse perspectives has amplified the voices of people who are marginalized, and has an enormous part to play in how we're all a lot more socially aware than older generations and other societies. So be careful to remember that not everyone has the capacity, time and resources available to embark on this journey. Having this access is very much a class privilege. It's important to share these resources when we have access to them.

This journey is going to be long and hard.

It will tie knots in your stomach as you visit the dark corners of your mind and discover you've held life-long beliefs about yourself and other people you weren't even aware of. Whenever I have a self-discovery breakthrough, I break *out*. Literally. My skin breaks out in spots – but I think those spots are beautiful. Each one of them represents my toxic behaviours, trauma, unhealthy coping mechanisms and long-held beliefs surfacing after *long* processing, ready to exit my body. It's a sign that I'm shedding another skin, preparing for my glow-up. Then off we go again...

Feminism is going to ruin your life, but in the best way.

No more watching your subconscious drive your life around for you while you sit in the passenger seat as it unfolds. You're going to take the wheel and drive it your damn self. Because silence and complacency in situations of injustice make you complicit in the violence.

Speak up.

Say something.

Your words have the power to change the fucking world.

FEELING GUILTY FOR PAST MISTAKES AND BEHAVIOURS DOES NOTHING FOR YOU OR THE PEOPLE YOU HARMED, UNLESS YOU USE IT TO CHANGE YOUR BEHAVIOUR.

CHAPTER 2

WOMEN DON'T OWE YOU PRETTY. BUT...

We live in a patriarchal society which prioritizes our desirability above anything and everything else.

Which means that...

Life is easier when we dress up.

Life is easier when we shave.

Life is easier when we wear make-up to work.

Life is easier when we have made a visible "effort" with our appearance.

Life is easier when we reflect society's idea of beauty. *Full stop.*

We are expected to show up and perform to expectations in order to be seen, and we know how to make our life easier if we apply the rules the patriarchy has set out for us. Look at where marginalized identities intersect with being a woman – trans women are still expected by society at large to perform this type of femininity to pass as a "real woman" (there's no such thing), and women of colour are expected by society to perform "prettiness" to a further degree, in a world where whiteness has been positioned as the epitome of beauty and "femininity". Historically there has been little representation of marginalized identities in the media and even when there is, it's often a stereotypical, harmful portrayal, constructing these identities as inferior to the default of whiteness, thinness and heterosexuality.

DESIRABILITY POLITICS — *AKA* "PRETTY PRIVILEGE"

Shaming other women for caring about their appearance is just another form of internalized misogyny, and an inability to see how race, class, sexuality and desirability all affect the way you're perceived in the world. In a world that prioritizes looks over everything else in women, and affords you undeserved privileges once you reflect its ideal standards of beauty, who are we to judge people who pay for aesthetic procedures to look this way? When, at the end of it, they are promised a better life and better treatment from other people the higher up they sit on the scale of desirability?

It would be wonderful if women didn't feel the need to go to extreme meaures just to posture their bodies in a "desirable enough" light, and could show up to work wearing no make-up without being told they're "looking a bit rough". But people still expect different levels of prettiness and desirability from women, depending on where they already sit in society's desirability hierarchy. We cannot shame people for using the tools around them to make their life easier and receive basic human respect. Whether that's a make-up brush or a razor, why would you want someone to suffer even more under the guise of having "superior feminist morals", when they're just trying to survive? We can't shame people for taking the steps and precautions that are expected of them just to be seen and heard in this messed-up world.

Different women experience different levels of expectation from society to perform femininity. Marginalized women such as trans women, fat women and women of colour don't always have the privilege of "rejecting beauty standards" such as growing out their armpit hair, or even wearing their natural hair that grows on their head. Because of our racist and fatphobic beauty standards – which subconsciously enforce our "preferences" when dating, hiring people, choosing friends – the way they are perceived just by existing in this world in their natural state is seen as "undesirable" and they are treated as "less than" already, *without* actively rebelling against gender norms.

> **Performing femininity and desirability isn't always a choice for marginalized women, it's often an act of survival.**

Have you ever thought about how differently you would experience the world if your appearance changed? If you cut off all your hair, if you stopped wearing make-up – would it make you feel *invisible? Or maybe you have already experienced this!* Think about your own privileges within these pre-set standards of desirability, and consider how they might have afforded you unearned benefits ahead of other people.

For example, one of my desirability privileges is that my whiteness is *already* perceived as "friendly" and "approachable" before I've even had a chance to speak or show people who I am. This subconsciously encourages people to open up to me and talk to me, enabling me more opportunities than women of colour, and Black women in particular, who are so often perceived initially as "intimidating" and "unapproachable" before people get to know them.

SHAVING

I stopped shaving my body the second I realized the reason I did it wasn't anything to do with my own discomfort, but was in fact entirely due to

LIFE IS TOO SHORT NOT TO LOVE THE SHIT OUT OF YOURSELF.

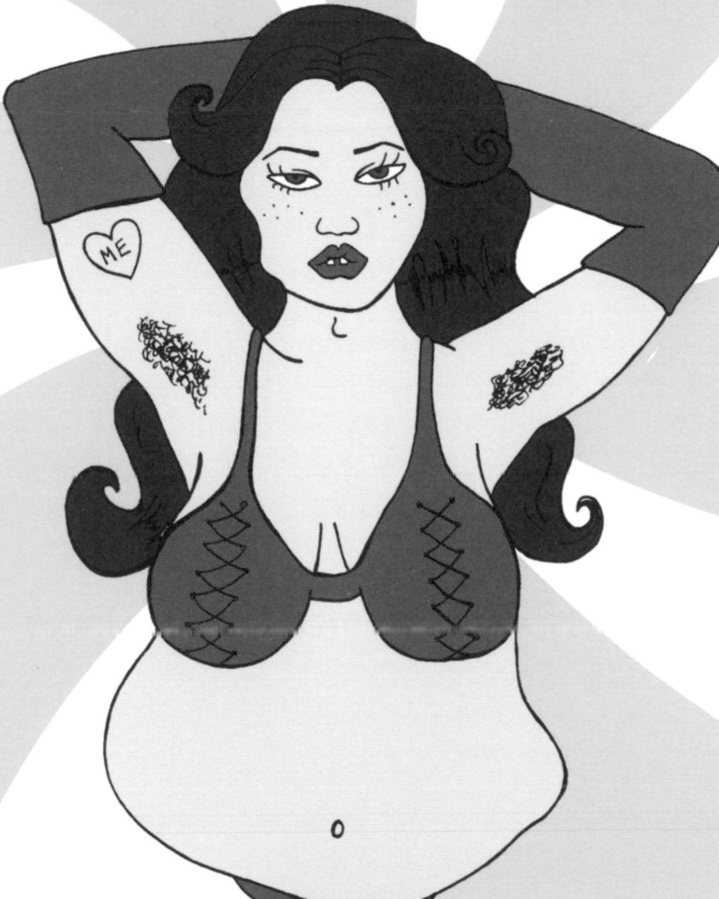

patriarchal brainwashing leading me to believe that my body hair was unattractive. I was fed up of being told that I should be repulsed by something that was part of my own body. I wanted to love my body, not hate her. As a survivor of sexual assault, I hate being told what to do with my body, and growing out my hair was a subtle and personal act of resistance and self-care that was instrumental to my healing process. It restored some of my autonomy, knowing that men and capitalism had no control over my body hair. *Fuck your overpriced pink razors, I'm gonna be a hairy bitch now!*

Growing out my armpit hair was a very intentional and conscious decision, but being able to grow out my body hair is in fact, a privilege. Sure, it's not viewed as desirable by the standards of the male gaze – most people still think it's repulsive and you will be shamed for it regardless of your race. But being able to grow out your body hair without facing *additional* discrimination is a privilege afforded only to thin, cisgender, white women like me. Because even with my armpit hair (which I can shave off any time I want) I will *still* be viewed as "desirable". And in a sexist, racist, capitalist society which places its value of women on their appearance and whether or not they're visually pleasing, having "natural" desirability is a *privilege* because you're more likely to be afforded opportunities, just for existing in the body that you do. I will still be viewed as "feminine" whether I shave or not, a privilege that not all trans women, fat women and women of colour have.

People compliment the hairs on my legs all the time, but complimenting people's body hair for being "blonde" and "fair" is a compliment at the *expense* of women of colour, whose body hair grows naturally much thicker and darker, often across their arms, upper lip, legs and brows. A lot of women of colour and trans women don't have the privilege of "forgetting" to shave or just letting it grow out, because they're constantly expected to show up in ways that people like me aren't to "prove" and perform femininity, in order to be met with the same respect I'm afforded as a woman, even when I don't do these things.

The ability to defiantly resist is only afforded to those who are already privileged enough not to be ostracized if they do so.

I don't know many trans women who grow out their leg or armpit hair, because they are held by society to much higher standards of "proving" their gender than cisgender women like myself are. Trans women don't owe it to anyone to perform their gender in a way that is hyper-feminine – but we must acknowledge that we live in a society that expects them to nonetheless, just as we expect women of colour to. There are double standards associated with our acceptance of body hair that cannot be ignored, and conversations around hair positivity need to centre around the voices of those whose bodies are most marginalized by society's expectations in the first place. It does not make you morally superior to grow out your body hair, and you're not any *less* of a feminist for shaving. Because let's face it, *life is easier when we shave*. Do what you want with your body hair! But remember that real change doesn't start until the people in the margins of our society are liberated and able to make the same decisions (without discrimination) that thin, non-disabled, cisgender, white people can already make.

RE-BRAINWASH YOURSELF!

To begin unpacking your own desirability bias and "preferences", you can start by listening to, learning from and respecting people you're *not* attracted to. If the content you consume is exclusively delivered to you by people you find palatable enough, thin enough, white enough, "nice" enough to listen to (aka – me) – then I'm going ask you to level up and

AS A WOMAN
IN THIS WORLD, IT
OFTEN FEELS AS THOUGH
WE HAVE TWO CHOICES:

WE CAN EITHER BE
DESIRED, OR RESPECTED.
SEEN, OR HEARD.

WE RARELY EVER GET
TO EXPERIENCE BOTH
AT THE SAME TIME.
WHICH ONE WE EXPERIENCE
OF COURSE, DEPENDS
ENTIRELY ON OUR
APPEARANCE.

challenge your *bland taste buds*. If you're only willing to hear one side of any argument, then you are fundamentally limiting your scope and ability to see beyond and above your own viewpoint.

Work on diversifying the content you consume. If you're constantly consuming and accessing the same media and content delivered by the same people – how are you ever going to open your mind to other people's perspectives, if it's always filtered through a privileged gaze?

Unfortunately, straight white men dominate our media, and the media is our cultural storyteller.

The media is what shapes our culture, so we have to make a conscious effort to break out of this cycle – it doesn't just happen.

Take action now. Read books by Black folks. Follow fat, disabled and trans people on Instagram.

We spend our whole lives being bombarded with *hetrifying* love stories, so follow queer couples on social media! Listen to podcasts created by people of colour on your way to work or, if you work from home, listen while you're working.

Up until now we have been bombarded with the same stories that either make us subconsciously hate ourselves or hate others. It's time to change the narrative, and the power lies in your hands. Consume diverse content. Reinvigorate those tired taste buds.

CHAPTER 3

YOU ARE THE LOVE OF YOUR OWN LIFE

One of the most radical acts under capitalism is to simply love yourself. Especially if the love you have cultivated for yourself is enough to fill you, without the need for romantic love to feel validated.

I often think how much the younger version of myself would have hated the person I am today. If the 14-year-old me had heard me saying the words "I am the love of my own life", I would have thought of myself as conceited, self-obsessed, selfish.

In fact, dear reader, you might be doing the very same right now.

The truth is that for a lot of people, it can be extremely uncomfortable to say nice, positive things about ourselves. For women in particular, we're taught that this makes us "vain". So when we hear others exude confidence it can remind us that we don't really value ourselves as highly as we should. We're forced to see the reality that deep down we don't really love ourselves, and to cope we might try to tear down the people who do. But with a shift in perspective, we're able to work on the relationship we have with ourselves, and stop projecting our hurt onto others.

We live in a world that profits from our insecurities, and it's often the patriarchal system that tells us we must settle for love, a kind of love that often lands us in the most emotionally debilitating and coercive relationships. Deciding that you deserve better is radical as hell, because you are actively going against centuries of social brainwashing and oppression; you are telling the world that you see through its bullshit. That you acknowledge it wants you to exist in one way (marry the first man to "sweep you off your feet" and have his kids...), but instead choosing to go your own way and make up your own damn rules.

A new person is born in the moment you say to yourself, for the first time, "I deserve better".

LIFE IS TOO SHORT NOT TO LOVE THE SHIT OUT OF YOURSELF

Most of the time, "self-love" and "self-care" are sold in a way that just further perpetuates the need for women to be constantly desirable and palatable. *Treat yourself! Buy this face mask! Pamper this! Pamper that! Shave your legs! Moisturize them! We're not trying to sell you anything – this is about you! It's self-care!* I don't know about you, but years of internalizing the messages about how women's bodies should look and the rigorous standards they're held to made me feel as though my body didn't belong to me – this *cannot* be eradicated by a stranger placing hot stones on my back. This kind of "self-love" takes me right back to square one – valuing myself based on the desirability of my face and body. While making myself up and feeling cute does bring me joy, it's only a temporary fix. It's instant short-term validation. It's a distraction.

I haven't learnt to love myself through a spa treatment, body wax or facial. Oh no. In fact, the journey started when, at 14, I lay in the middle of the busy park that all the girls from my school frequented, and tried my hardest not to give a shit what any of them thought of me. I told myself that if I could lie there and listen to *one song*, without caring what anyone thought, I could do literally *anything*. This was a big moment. My biggest fear was being judged by others and I needed to conquer it. I was in an emotionally abusive co-dependent friendship with a girl who later isolated me from our entire friendship group after hearing rumours about my eating disorder. I had a lot of social anxiety. I feared looking like "a loner". I feared having to discover who I was, outside of serving someone else's needs – because the truth was I had no idea. But because I'd been exiled from their friendship group, I was left with no choice but to find out.

So, lying in that park alone scared me, but it also unshackled me from living a life restricted by other people's perceptions. It's not their bullying that "made me the person I am today", but my own resilience that enabled me to adapt. I had stepped out of my comfort zone, and entered the world of *living*. I had a taste of what my life could look like if I truly denounced the need to be liked. If I hadn't made the decision to lie in that park, I wouldn't be writing this book today, because I wouldn't have found the courage to unapologetically voice my opinions. The ability to do so was born in that moment. *Full stop.*

Think about something you wish you could do. What is it that's stopping you from pursuing it? Do you hate the thought of being alone in public, or is it the perception you imagine *other people* have about you being alone? It sure was the latter for me. The idea of being out on my own? Bliss. The idea of people seeing me out on my own? Hell. I *revelled* in my alone time, but I was afraid of being judged by others for being on my own.

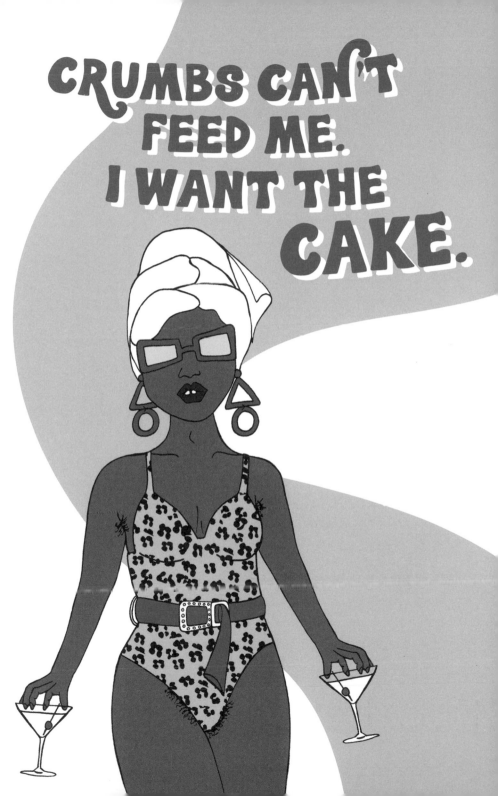

It's the same principle with my body hair. I'd been shaving it religiously for years, only to realize that the sight of it wasn't making *me* feel uncomfortable, it was the thought of making others feel uncomfortable if *they* saw it. My fear of others' opinions on the hair that grows naturally out of my body (just as men's hair, which society deems socially acceptable, does) made me take a razor blade to my armpit and leg hair every single week.

Making these autonomous decisions is tricky because it means breaking life-long habits. It can be further complicated by your identity intersections in society, and by your class privilege, ability privilege, sexuality privilege, race privilege, cisgender privilege, etc. Our lives as women are already so restricted in terms of what we can and can't do because of the safety measures we're forced to take – living our lives constantly vigilant and compromising our comfort for our safety in public – so why should we self-impose *further* limitations around what we can and can't do?

The truth is that no one is ever looking at you and thinking "what the hell are they doing on their own?". Most of the time the things we are insecure about aren't about *our* dislike towards them, but what we think *others* will think when they see us. But no one actually cares because they are wrapped up in their own dialogue. If you've never done it before, promise me you will take yourself on a date. Don't take your laptop, don't use your phone, go completely and entirely alone with no other purpose than to simply eat, drink and watch the world go by. Life is far too short to be waiting around for someone to ask you. You are the love of your own life, so act accordingly and take your damn self out.

PATRIARCHY WANTS YOU TO SETTLE. DON'T.

As a society, we have such an odd way of pitching and positioning single women. The way we talk to women approaching their thirties is often as though at any given moment, if they don't couple up, they might actually *combust*. We tell them that they need to get their skates on and pressure them to act soon while they're "young and beautiful". The fact that a lot of women fear being single has a lot to do with the language surrounding relationships. We talk of women being the "last one on the shelf", people in couples talk of their partners as their "other half" as though being single means they're incomplete. Heteronormativity has truly fucked up so many of us, to the point where we would rather be in a toxic relationship than have no relationship at all. Heteronormativity wants women to *settle*.

Heteronormativity has convinced us all that being single is some kind of tragic fate, as though we have been thrust unwillingly into a state of "waiting for the next relationship", a state which we must get ourselves out of immediately. I changed the way I viewed being single when I flipped my perspective. I realized it was a *choice.* You're choosing to be single, you also might have turned down some people since your last relationship, and that in itself is you actively deciding that you'd rather be *on your own* than settle for less than you deserve. You have set your standards and, by staying single, you're sticking to them. You have decided that you deserve quality treatment (whatever that means to you) and anything that does not seek to add value to your life doesn't deserve a place in it. Simple! Knowing what you'd want from a partner, new friend or even your career can be so powerful. Because when situations and people which *do not* align with what you want and need present themselves, they can be intentionally avoided.

They're just a distraction.

Carry on, as you were.

"Single" doesn't mean "waiting for someone".

Choosing to be single is an autonomous choice, and a lot of men fear autonomous women and gender non-conforming people. It reminds them that we have other purposes on this planet than to serve them. Women who don't have kids are called "selfish" and made to feel that their

THEY'RE JUST A
DISTRACTION.
CARRY ON,
AS YOU WERE.

life is a waste. Women in heterosexual relationships who earn more than their partners are labelled "controlling" or "bossy". Women who reject sexual advances are called "frigid", yet that same accuser will call a woman who enjoys casual sex a "slut". When people make autonomous decisions about their bodies and their lifestyles they are met with a whole spectrum of resistance and this is particularly true for marginalized people. Anything that deviates from the narrative society has written for and about you is shamed and unaccepted.

In a society that punishes you either way, the only option is to do what makes *you* happy.

Do you prioritize your romantic life over your own mental health, friendships and the relationship you have with yourself?

> **If you could stop worrying about romantic love altogether, what would you be able to achieve with this new, enormous resource of energy?**

STOP SETTLING FOR CRUMBS, YOU DESERVE THE WHOLE DAMN CAKE

What are crumbs, you ask?

Crumbs are the *audaciously* small tokens and gestures that people throw us, in order to keep us under the illusion that they deserve a place in our lives – despite bringing very little (or no) value to it. We often allow this kind of behaviour because our low self-esteem leads us to believe that this is the kind of love we deserve, and over time it becomes normalized to us. When we continue to accept crumbs from someone, it enables them to dip back into our lives when they're bored and treat us like a doormat because technically, no one "closed the door".

Crumbs can be any of the following:
- Text messages
- Liking your Instagram pictures
- Replying/reacting to your Instagram stories
- Hitting you up randomly with a "wyd" text
- Saying things out of the blue that they know will fluff your ego.
- Dropping back in after a period of ghosting. (When they're running low on self-esteem, you're their "hit" to make themselves feel better.)

You'll notice most of the "interactions" I have listed occur online. That's because someone who gives you crumbs doesn't have any *actual* time for you IRL. Because, *surprise!* They don't value you. It's hard to hear I know, but they value only what you can do for their own ego. If they do "make time" for you, you can bet it will *always* be when it suits them. During late hours, when they're bored, or when the person who makes them work for attention isn't texting *them* back. They know they can rely on you to boost them back up. This person will keep throwing you just enough crumbs to make sure they never lose that spot in your life, but not enough to the point of actually spending any of their energy, investing any of their time or reciprocating the energy you give so freely and instinctively to them.

The *moment* someone shows the audacity of trying to keep you around for an exchange of crumbs, communicate to them that you want the whole cake (i.e. that you want to be taken out on a proper date/build a relationship with this person). If they say they can't give it to you, that they're not ready to give you the cake, or they promise they can give you the cake at a later date, leave them where they're at and move the hell on.

Promise yourself to stop buying into people's potential.

You're not a start-up investor.

When you settle for crumbs it sends a message to that person that that's all you think you deserve. They know that they can get away with doing the absolute bare minimum to have a seat at your table. That they can come and go as they please – for the price of their mere *attention*. They've become a parasite, and you're their host.

But my love, you deserve better than that. Depending on our "desirability", our childhood experiences, friendships, relationships and trauma, we all received different messages about what kind of love we deserve. Please know that no matter what you've been told to believe about yourself, the toxic kind of love you've learned to "accept", or whatever it is that society has brainwashed you into believing, you are *no one's* fucking doormat. You are not a source of energy for others to take. This is *your* table, *you* set the standards and *you* choose who gets a seat. Start turning away people who have the audacity to show up in your life with crumbs, because crumbs can't feed you. Find someone who brings you a whole cake.

Learning how to love yourself, to avoid relying on other people's validation to make you feel whole, is the *key* to not settling. *You've got to learn to make the cake yourself.* Because when you already have a delicious fucking cake, the idea of someone else's crumbs and settling for a mediocre love that leaves you starving ceases to be tempting. You must live your life as if no one is ever going to make you a cake. Don't sit around waiting for someone to give you the cake. Bake it yourself. Start from scratch. Add ingredients to the cake. Experiment with your cake. Write your name all over the cake in vanilla fucking frosting and cover it in your favourite toppings. This is how you refuse to settle for less than you deserve! You ensure that you have everything you could possibly need, *supplied to and from yourself*.

The process of being single and dating to me is very much like making my own cake. Refining the recipe, learning which ingredients I like the taste of and which spoil the mix, so that I will always have enough to fill and satisfy my desires without the aid of someone else.

You are the love of your own life. Make your own cake.

CHAPTER 4

HOW TO BREAK UP WITH YOURSELF

Growth involves breaking up with *yourself*. (That's what makes it so bloody uncomfortable.)

We have become all too attached to our suffering strategies, to the narratives we keep telling ourselves and to repeating self-sabotaging behaviour. We find it easier to blame others and the world around us than to question how much of our pain is caused by subconsciously *choosing* this suffering, because it's a lovely, familiar state of being.

An example of a comfortable, self-sabotaging narrative that I have indulged in myself: "I'm such an empath, my positive energy attracts people into my life who just want to use me." As long as you keep telling yourself this, it will keep happening and people will continue to use you if the narrative you believe is that bad people "wander" into your life because you're a healing, empathic, positive person. This is comfortable for you, because it means you don't have to change. But sticking to this way of thinking just prolongs your suffering. Yes, you might very well be an empath, and no one deserves abuse, or to be used as a resource – but you *also* need to hold yourself accountable for the ways you might

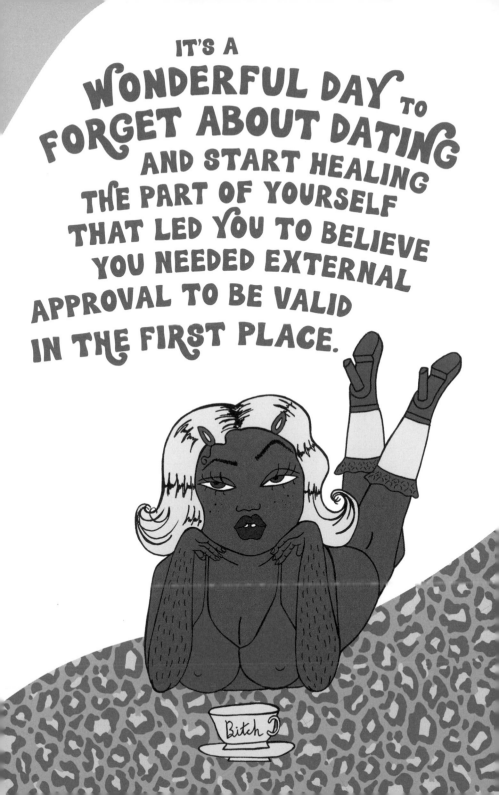

SOMETIMES THE PERSON STOPPING YOU FROM REACHING YOUR POTENTIAL ALL ALONG WAS YOUR OWN SUBCONSCIOUS ADDICTED TO THE COMFORT THAT COMES FROM BLAMING OTHERS.

IT'S TIME TO GET OUT OF YOUR OWN WAY.

be inserting yourself into other peoples' lives and trying to fix them. You need to question whether the reason people keep using you is because you don't know your worth outside of being able to fix other people. So, subconsciously, you surround yourself with broken people and energy parasites because they make you feel needed. Without them you might feel useless, because you never experienced/were exposed to examples of a healthy reciprocal love as a child...Maybe.

As humans, we don't really want to find out whether any of our suffering has to do with *us*. After all, who would *choose* suffering? But growth requires accountability, and accountability is questioning whether "bad people" might actually be wandering into your life because they're attracted to your lack of boundaries, and staying in your life because you're afraid of conflict. The kind of love you *accept* into your life is a reflection of the love that deep down you think you *deserve*. Low self-esteem doesn't mean you deserve bad treatment, accountability is not about victim blaming (see page 192). Accountability shows you what parts of yourself need healing. Questioning and interrogating yourself is paramount in escaping these destructive patterns and cycles of behaviour.

In order to grow, you have to thank your old self, trust you deserve better, say goodbye and move on.

You have to be willing to accept that sometimes you are *self*-sabotaging. Pointing the finger at those around you isn't going to bring about real and lasting change. You have to be held accountable for growth, you have to be willing to alter your perception and break up with the version of yourself that you have been clinging to for so long. You have to say goodbye to that former self-protective shell and accept that it played its role in your life, in survival mode. But you have now outgrown it, and you need to build a better, bigger version for you to evolve into the person you are becoming.

CHAPTER 5

REFUSE TO FIND COMFORT IN OTHER WOMEN'S FLAWS

Internalized misogyny is the silent, insidious killer of progress, and when it shows up in our lives it can make us act out in all kinds of ugly ways.

First things first, "flaws" aren't really there. Flaws are man-made. And yes, I mean *man*-made.

They're seeds planted in our minds by manipulative power systems, to make us feel so insecure that we buy products that promise we will become more acceptable, more desirable and physically attractive. The beauty standards of our society are racist, fatphobic, ageist and quite frankly, confusing. The things you feel most insecure about in your body are more than likely a direct result of capitalism because it works very hard to make sure that you will never feel enough without the aid of its products. The models we see promoting these products and advertising this image of perceived flawlessness don't even look like that themselves. Their skin has been airbrushed, their bodies manipulated and their features enhanced. In a lot of cases, Black women's skin is lightened and their features dramatically altered in post-production to make them look more European and perpetuate the colonial idea that whiteness equates with beauty.

As a result of the rigorous beauty standards that we are so harshly held up against, we inevitably find a disturbing amount of comfort in tearing down women who reflect our insecurities *back to us*. We are distracted by capitalism's ability to manipulate us because it is hidden in the promise of "becoming more beautiful", which actually just means becoming more desirable for male consumption. This creates a toxic competitiveness among women, in a pursuit to fill the void caused by insecurities and these toxic standards of beauty. Capitalism profits from the insecurities it is responsible for creating in the first place and it is entirely exploitative. How can we happily exist in a world which is built on systems that seek to tear us down?

The internalized misogynist will tell you that women shouldn't do "certain things" because of this sexist narrative that society has laid out for us. I used to hate the *shit* out of hot, confident bisexual women. Why? Because I was jealous that they got to live their truth! It was so threatening and frightening to my heteronormative understanding of my own sexuality. Seeing them thrive and dating whoever they wanted – how *dare* they. They were everything I wanted to be but couldn't, because I had placed limitations on my own sexuality due to this internalized biphobia. Instead of dealing with the fact that I was bisexual myself, I projected the shame around my sexuality onto the women who were confident enough to own it. I hated that these women were living the life I wanted, but I didn't realize that was the reason until I had finally accepted and embraced my own sexuality.

Once you heal your insecurities, get to the root of where they originate and identify the parts of yourself that you're ashamed of, you reframe your perspective of others and open the door to a wonderful thing called *empathy*.

It is through years of retraining that I have minimized the power internalized misogyny has over my thoughts. I realized that judging other women is usually just a quick way to get out of dealing with the things we dislike about *ourselves*. We seek comfort in other women's perceived "flaws" in an attempt to avoid addressing our own insecurities. The things that have been planted in our minds keep us competing with each other, preventing us from growing and discovering our innate divine power – this is the patriarchy's main goal.

Every time you catch yourself critiquing a woman on the choices she makes – who she sleeps with, how she dresses – sit in it. Reflect. What is it about her that makes you feel so uncomfortable? Perhaps she actually just reminds you of yourself, or the parts of yourself that you are ashamed of. Or perhaps she's the very person you *want to be*. Sometimes we dislike women simply because they're making the bold choices that we are too afraid to make ourselves, the choices that society has made us feel are wrong or shameful because they go against the patriarchal narrative. Or perhaps you're like me – you actually just really fancy her and need to go *ask her out*.

Ask yourself why you think this way, instead of just accepting it. Reprogramme your patriarchal brainwashing. The girl you're jealous and hateful of isn't a "bitch", your internalized misogynist is.

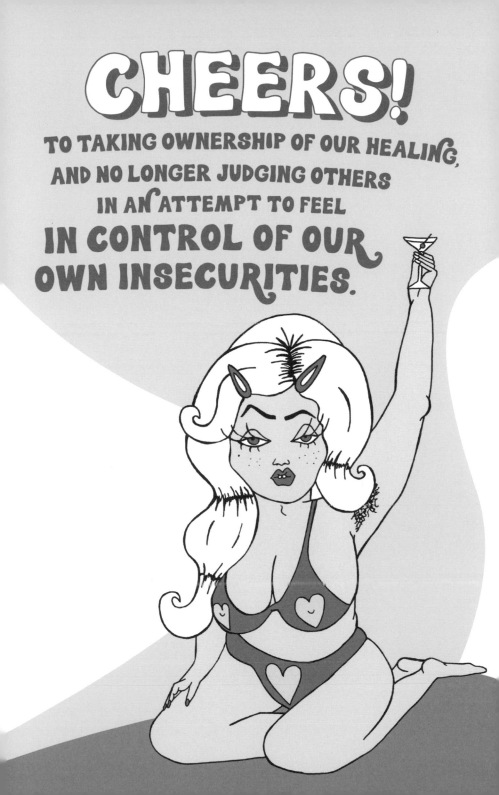

EXAMPLES OF INTERNALIZED MISOGYNY

Here are some key examples of what internalized misogyny looks like, and how to handle it when she rocks up in your brain:

You find yourself saying "I'm not like the other girls."

What are you implying the other girls "are like"? If you are reinforcing stereotypes that women are "bitchy" or "full of drama" and that you are the exception, darling, *you are not.* You're literally sat there bitching like the "rest of us"! Stereotypes sit at the bottom of a pyramid and they fuel the bigger problems at the top, such as gendered physical violence towards women (it sounds dramatic, but it isn't). Don't perpetuate the cycle. Stop trying to please men by shaming other women. It's never worked.

You constantly find ways to tear down successful women.

We truly despise people who remind us of the parts of our lives we wish we were thriving in, but aren't. "Who the hell does she think she is?!" "I don't like her. I can't put my finger on it, I just don't." "She's so annoying. She's changed since she's become successful." Be careful not to fall into the habit of tearing down other women to make yourself feel better. The satisfaction will wear off and you'll be back facing those unaddressed insecurities that you need to work on. That's on you, it's your responsibility. Leave her alone, let her shine!

No, you don't have to like *all* women – don't put that pressure on yourself. You do not have to uplift, empower or make friends with someone who you don't get on with just because they are a woman. But, depending on our privileges there are times where we should be giving up space, to further marginalized women. The key is to learn to recognize whether the problem is actually her, or if it's your own insecurities. Take note of the things that make you want to tear her down. A big old red flag to look out for is if you catch yourself taking even a *little* comfort in her pain, unhappiness, or "bad days" on social media. If seeing someone's low moments eases your anxiety and makes you feel like you're "winning", work on it. For example, are you jealous that she's running a thriving business? Go home, write a list of all the things that bring you joy and figure out ways to start making a profit. Are you pissed that she has lots of cool, like-minded friends? My love, use the internet! Follow pages with your interests and try to build an online community of like-minded people that you could potentially meet IRL. Is she always pulling incredible looks, is her make-up on point? Start watching those YouTube tutorials! Does the fact that she has a similar style irritate you? Great minds think alike, why not pitch a collaboration instead?

If we can learn to view other women as opportunities for inspiration and empowerment in our own lives and realize that there is enough room for *all of us* to be happy, the relationships and bonds we form together will be unstoppable.

You hate your partner's ex.

Being in a relationship with someone who has an ex-girlfriend is the perfect opportunity to wrestle through our internalized misogyny. This is possibly the most heightened that our internalized hatred of other women can ever become. Why? Because we literally put ourselves in an imaginary competition with our partner's ex. And with social media being a 24/7 accessible window into someone's life you'll probably catch yourself stalking her for hours on end – comparing yourself to every single aspect of her life or, worse yet, actively trying to seek out flaws for temporary relief to make yourself feel better. It's awful, and it's ugly. If it gets to the point where you start picking fights with your partner over her because of your insecurities, try to remember that it's not on them, this is on you.

But don't worry, you've got this. It's a great opportunity for you to work on strengthening the love you have for yourself and, as a result, other women! It's so easy to blame other women because, well – everyone blames women! We are constantly used as the scapegoats to justify other people's actions. So maybe you need to also question whether the reason you're so worried about their ex is because the person you're with just isn't the one for you. As soon as I dumped my ex all the petty resentment I'd built up towards the women he had a history with, dissipated. It made me realize that he was the problem all along. He brought out a nasty jealous aspect in me, and life's too short to be around people who make you feel like you need to compete for their attention. If that's the case, just dump them. Don't waste time with someone who doesn't acknowledge that you are walking divinity, darling.

You say "she's a slut."
Or is she actually just getting on with her life and exercising her right to bodily autonomy? Regardless, it's none of your business.

Ask yourself if you would say the same thing about a man. These pernicious stereotypes are largely saved for women, and when we bad-mouth other women for expressing their sexuality, we feed into the narrative that women have no agency over their bodies. Whatever women choose to do with their sex lives, it's never your business. In a society that turns women into objects, who are you to judge people that find empowerment in the very narrative that tries to demean their human existence?

You say "she's so bossy and intimidating!"
When a woman asserts her boundaries and says "no" to things, she's not being bossy. She is doing exactly what she has to do to protect her energy and GET. SHIT. DONE. Ask yourself this question: "is she intimidating, or am I intimidated?" (see page 66).

Is she bossy or is she just acting outside of the submissive-woman stereotype that society has convinced you she needs to be – instruction-taking, submissive, docile? Women are socialized to constantly pander to the needs of everyone else but themselves, and even if we do decide to take care of ourselves, we are encouraged to do it in the form of "retail therapy" or "facials", still pandering to our appearance instead of our mental health, giving money to products that tell us we exist only to be desired and good looking.

Respect women who set firm boundaries, don't see it as a threat. She's worked really fucking hard to get to a point in her life where she has decided to choose her happiness over people-pleasing. When you see women acting outside of their gendered stereotype, remind yourself that there is no one way to be a woman, and tell your internalized misogynist to shut the hell up! Gender roles are socially constructed and we are allowed to behave as closely, or as far away from them, as we wish.

Maybe she's a "bitch", or maybe her ability to unapologetically set boundaries makes you uncomfortable, because it forces you to acknowledge that you are a doormat to everyone in your life.

...Maybe.

You judge other women on their appearance.
When my own judgmental thoughts show up, I flip them around and say the opposite. Empower others instead of judging them – practising empathy can change the world. For example:

- You see a woman walking down the street in a miniskirt and your immediate thought is that she should be dressing "more carefully". Flip it around; instead say, "Her clothes aren't the problem, the problem is rapists and their predatorial behaviour towards women's bodies."
- You see an older woman rocking a tight dress she ordered off ASOS in the club and your first thought is, *Bloody hell!*

She's too old for that!". Flip it around: instead say, "Wow, *in spite* of ageism and the sexist idea that women past a certain age shouldn't love and flaunt their bodies, this woman decided to just go for it anyway! What a fucking legend."

- You see a woman who covers herself up (for religious or non-religious purposes, neither of which are your business) and your immediate assumption is that she must be "prudish" and "unempowered". Flip it around: instead say, "Different things empower different people – there is no one way to be a woman. Women are multifaceted human beings capable of being more than one thing at the same time."

- You either treat butch women/masc women with less respect or you make remarks about their appearance because of their lack of femininity. Flip it around: instead say "wow, in spite of the expectation for women to constantly cater their appearance to the male gaze and the privileges that come with this, these butch ICONS are choosing to express their gender in a way that feels most authentic to themselves".

- You judge or pity divorced women. Flip it around: think to yourself "divorced women are *actually* iconic. They successfully escaped a situation in which they were unhappily trapped. I hope I have the courage to do the same if I ever find myself in a similar situation."

- You make comments on Black women's hair, or use words such as "bossy" or "aggressive" to describe Black women in power. Any unsolicited comments on how Black women choose to live their life or carry themselves is both misogynistic and racist. Full stop.

I could go on forever. But when it comes to judging other people, ask yourself if what they are doing is affecting you. If it isn't, we must learn to move the fuck on with our lives. If we want to battle through internalized sexism and our constant urge to judge women on their appearance, we must be willing to challenge it when it pops up in our minds.

THERE IS ENOUGH ROOM FOR ALL WOMEN TO BE WHOLE WITHOUT TEARING EACH OTHER DOWN.

You judge other women who pay for aesthetic procedures.
In a society that affords *undeserved* privileges once you reflect its beauty standards, we cannot judge, criticize or shame other women who pay to make themselves look this way. The media is saturated with hyper-feminine, objectifying portrayals of female characters. We can't take the effect and make it the cause. Wouldn't it be incredible if we lived in a world where women didn't feel the need to adhere to sexist beauty standards, and go under the knife? You're goddamn right it would. But that world doesn't yet exist. Which is why we must fight to make it exist, instead of blaming women for trying to thrive within the framework that is currently on offer.

You find yourself saying things like "she looks good for her age".
Ageism is a heavily gendered issue. It seems that any woman past the age of 25 has an urgency placed on her by society to rush and find a husband before she's "old, wrinkly and infertile".

When was the last time you heard of a man exclaiming that he *must* find a bride before he gets old and grey? When have you heard a man get excited over finding a bride? Men are taught to put themselves first, and it's about time we were encouraged to do the same. There is a societal time limit placed on women, as our value as human beings is tied to our physical "beauty". The older we get, the less valuable we are to society. We are deemed worthless if we are neither fertile nor "beautiful" in the eyes of the male gaze (see page 150). The next time you find yourself commenting on a woman in relation to her appearance, abilities or God forbid her fertility, stop. Ask yourself if you would say the same thing about a man.

If you have ever caught yourself thinking or experiencing these thoughts, I suggest you give these intrusive thoughts a name. And then tell them that they don't belong in your mind or life, because they're ruining your relationship with other women.

MAYBE IT'S TENSION, MAYBE YOU'RE PROJECTING

Do you ever find yourself talking about other people to your friends and create this whole narrative in your head that they "have it in for you" or that they hate you? Even though you've had little or no communication with this person at all? Well, they don't hate you! You just hate *yourself!*

The only person "judging you" is yourself. They are holding a mirror up to your insecurities, and you can't handle it. Stop shaming that girl in the club who's dancing her tits off in a short dress and living her best life – and go bloody join her! Stop assuming that confident women hate *you* just because they love *themselves.* She isn't your competition, this isn't about her, it's about you. It's a big thing to be able to admit your own shortcomings and actively work to stop your own insecurities affecting other people. Try as often as possible to operate your thoughts from a non-judgemental place, and catch yourself when you do this. We all do it, we're all human.

> **Your character is not to be judged by the mistakes you make — but your ability to hold yourself accountable, interrogate your actions and come back with the correct behaviour.**

HOW SHOULD YOU DEAL WITH WOMEN WHO INFLICT MISOGYNY ONTO *YOU?*

It can be incredibly hard to experience the wrath of the patriarchy at the hands of another woman, but remember that *everyone* internalizes sexism. We all live in the same society and internalize the same messages. The way they are treating you is not a reflection of you or your character, but of their own internal dialogue. If someone is judging you, try to empathize with them instead. Try to see that they are hurting and that the way they are talking to you is a projection of how they feel about themselves.

Let's break the cycle of abuse.

CHAPTER 6

ARE THEY INTIMIDATING, OR AM I INTIMIDATED?

The way people treat you is absolutely no reflection of you, your worth or your value.

Anything that anyone ever says to you is, in the words of Dr Thema, "based on a *projection* of how they feel about themselves and their *assumptions* of you". These assumptions will be based on a whole host of biases, from racism, transphobia, homophobia etc and also their own insecurities. This is not to excuse people's shitty behaviour, but if you can master the art of not internalizing other people's insecurities (aka not giving a shit what people think or say about you), you will live a much more peaceful, authentic life.

It can be hard to fully accept that what people are saying to you is not a reflection of you, but of them. But we need to get out of the habit of internalizing other people's insecurities and society's harmful messaging. To make it less personal, I want you to try to remove yourself and think about how people project themselves, their experiences and their preferences onto art.

The perfect example of projection is how people can interpret the same piece of artwork in many different ways, based on their different lived experiences, tastes and where they're at in their life. Because art is subjective. Art is a form of human expression, a way of connecting to the people who consume it, a way to open people's minds, or create something to look at, stimulate and observe thought. Art is usually a reflection of our inner truth and sharing this work can make us feel quite vulnerable. It feels like an extension of ourselves. I used to take criticism so personally for this reason, because my artwork is quite literally an amalgamation of my experiences and personal style, churned out for the world to see in the form of illustrations and essays so other people can learn from my mistakes. It can make us feel *very* vulnerable and exposed.

But my perspective changed completely when I realized that no matter what anyone says about your art, *the art remains the same*. It doesn't actually change! It blew my damn mind. Your perception of it may have changed, but the art itself has stayed the same the whole time.

When people say cruel things, consider what is said, but also who is saying it, and where that criticism might originate, what it might be rooted in.

If I hadn't learned that people bring their own insecurities and prejudices to their critiques about others, and had instead taken their criticism as *objective feedback*, I wouldn't be making art for myself anymore. I'd be a people-pleasing puppet, allowing other people's inner turmoil to dictate the work I was creating.

When I first started putting out my politically charged artwork on the internet at the age of 17, it felt like I was carving out a piece of my mind and laying it bare for everyone to

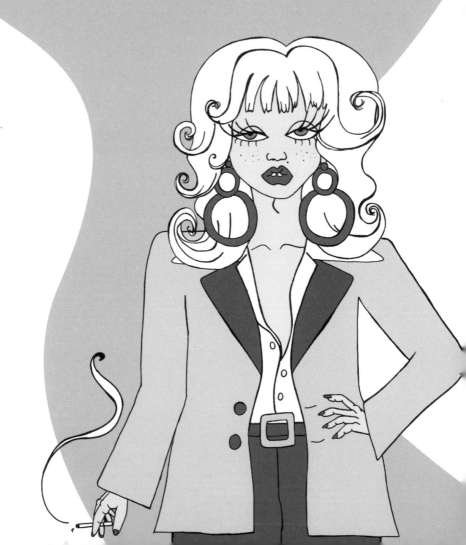

see on a surgical trolley. I felt vulnerable, uncomfortable and exposed. But only for a second, and that discomfort was worth it. More and more women gradually came forward telling me that they related to the experiences I was discussing, and before I knew it I had created a small community of people wanting to feel empowered, shedding the shame they had been carrying for simply existing in this world. If I didn't choose to leave my comfort zone and be loud about the things I care about, I wouldn't be writing this book and I wouldn't have embarked on the greatest journey of my life.

If someone tells you that you're "too much" – it's because they don't feel *enough*. If someone tells you that you're "too sensitive", it's because deep down they *envy* your ability to be vulnerable, your capacity to feel and the freedom you give yourself to express your feelings. Hurt people, hurt people.

> **"Stop breaking yourself down into bite-sized pieces. Stay whole and let them choke."**
> **— maybeinaparalleluniverse.tumblr.com**

PEOPLE-PLEASING — STOP WANTING TO BE LIKED

Choosing yourself will always disappoint some people. The sooner we accept this and make peace with it, the better.

People who do not know themselves and don't have a strong sense of self will constantly change to reflect their surroundings and the people they are with. People-pleasers change who they are constantly, and each time they do this it's like they silence an authentic part of themselves to be something else, for *someone* else. We are all multifaceted human beings and we choose to show different sides of ourselves to our parents, our co-workers, friends and romantic partners. For a lot of marginalized people, "code switching" and learning to assimilate to the dominant culture (white, straight, cis) is a part of survival, in order to be met with basic human respect. Just as women have learned to perform femininity. That's not to say this is fair – it isn't.

Compromising or adopting parts of your identity, beliefs and personality to be liked by someone is neither healthy nor sustainable, and quite frankly it's *exhausting*. Performing patriarchal beauty standards and being a woman is exhausting enough, so why give yourself the added pressure of another layer of performance? You cannot win, and the world will judge you either way. Feel empowered and not defeated by this truth – it means that the only available option is to be *yourself*.

Compromising to form relationships and friendships doesn't work because they will be based on a false connection. Present *exactly* what you want and need, and if they can't match it then at least you know. They were never for you, and that's okay.

Get over the need to please everyone you meet. Start living for yourself.

You need a strong sense of self to maintain healthy relationships. People in long-term relationships can often over time find themselves merging, and it can become very hard to distinguish parts of yourself from your partner, to the point of self-neglect. You forget what your own interests are and stop doing things for yourself. I've been there, and it was one of the reasons I dumped him. I realized that I'd drifted too far from myself in raising a man-child and trying to grow someone else's potential. I wanted a partner, not a child that I had to *raise*. This is why it's important to make yourself the love of your life, first (see page 40). If you do not know yourself or your boundaries, you'll be constantly looking for other people to tell you who you are. Self-discovery and self-reflection, facing the darkest parts and becoming a more refined version of ourselves, is beneficial to every aspect of our lives.

DON'T PROJECT BACK WHAT HAS BEEN PROJECTED ONTO YOU

Painful things happen. Whatever shit situation you have found yourself in was not your fault. But if we leave past experiences unchecked, we can

WHEN YOU HAVE LIVED A LIFE OF PEOPLE PLEASING SAYING YOUR TRUE DESIRES WILL MAKE YOU FEEL GUILTY. PUSH THROUGH AND COMMUNICATE THEM. YOU DIDN'T COME HERE TO BE LIKED.

end up unintentionally inflicting the same pain onto other people as a coping mechanism. In fact, it's very likely that the pain that was inflicted onto you in the first place was a direct result of someone who hadn't dealt with *their* own issues (domestic violence, absent parent in childhood, bullying...). This explains what happened to you but it does not excuse it. We are all responsible for our own healing, and it's in your power how you choose to let it impact your life and those close around you. You have to be responsible for the way you treat others, despite what has happened to you. It is your responsibility not to project your trauma, past experiences and insecurities onto other people.

This is not victim blaming, this is accountability.

Sometimes projection manifests itself physically. People build entire lives, spin false narratives and accumulate material possessions all because of their insecurities or guilt. They feel the need to fill their void, when what they really need is therapy. We all have insecurities, but it is our responsibility not to inflict them on others and cause further suffering.

The next time you think about commenting on someone's appearance, catch yourself and consider why you feel the need to do this. Is it to make you feel more in control of your own life? Ask yourself if you really need to insert yourself into this situation. What good will it do, except reveal to everyone around you that you're an insecure or ignorant person? Keep your unwarranted commentaries about other people's lives to yourself, work through why you feel the need to gossip about others in the first place, heal those wounds and come back with correct behaviour.

I hate engaging in spiteful gossip, so if one of my friends starts to tell me something I don't want to hear about, I try to say, "That's not our business, let's not be *those* people." It holds a mirror to that person and gently asks them to reflect. Not everyone takes this easily, especially as gossip is one of the things women are encouraged to "bond" over. You'll often be met with a defensive reaction from friends, but this person has been faced with their truth (that gossiping is ugly and a reflection of their inner reality) and will say anything to make you the problem for not wanting to gossip. You want to get to a point in your life where gossiping is genuinely unenjoyable. I no longer enjoy forming bonds with people at the expense of exchanging information about other people's lives. If I find myself slipping into that mindset with a new friend, which I have many times, it's a red flag. They bring out a bad side of me. It isn't healthy, and it says more about how you view yourself than the qualities of the person in discussion. Surround yourself with people who have an open mind, people that are open to learning from you, and people whose perspectives you are open to listening to also. We all mess up every now and then, but you must remember to do the work yourself rather than leaning on other people to teach you. Other people's spiteful projections will cease to hold any power over the way you view yourself if you can relinquish your grasp on their meaning. Let go. It's not about you.

Think back to a time when you said something you didn't believe in, for the temporary satisfaction that another person would feel connected to you. Analyze *why* you did this, and babe – *don't do that shit again.*

For example, one of the times that I shrunk myself down for approval was at the beginning of my feminist journey, by "dampening down" my feminism around men. I would water down my ideas and feel disgusted at myself, as I found that their reaction to my watered-down feminism was feeding my internalized misogynist, making myself out to be "not like those other feminists" for their temporary approval.

When it's safe to, being your authentic self forces people to reveal whether they deserve a place in your life or not. This truth is a *gift* and will save you a lot of energy. Stop breaking down. Stay whole.

CHAPTER 7

STOP SCROLLING IN THE MORNINGS

If it wasn't for social media:

- I wouldn't know some of my closest friends
- I would not be "out" as a queer woman (at least, not at this stage in my life)
- I would not have the chance to meet and date lots of queer people
- I would not have found the tools to spot abusive behaviours in relationships
- I would not have got myself into therapy
- I would not have been given the opportunity to write the book you are reading

These are just a few powerful ways that social media has positively impacted my life, and how I have harnessed its vast catalogue of information and perspectives to liberate myself from toxic situations, and embark on my journey of growth and understanding myself.

As someone whose IRL community was non-existent, I was aching for conversations that challenged me and my perception of reality. To put it simply, *I despised stagnancy and I craved growth*. I still do. I got a taste of that when I started to vocalize my experiences and my opinions online. I couldn't believe there were other teenagers out there as fed up with the same bullshit as I was, but that there were also voices I'd never heard from before or come across in the world I inhabited – people whose perspectives would become invaluable to my understanding of not just the systems of oppression that I was suffering under, but ones that I benefitted from too. Influencers, educators, therapists and artists online have taught me more valuable lessons about the world and *myself* than I was ever afforded during my formal education in school. Instagram creators filled all the overlooked but important gaps in my education, highlighting the importance of emotional intelligence and empathy.

Social media amplified the voices of marginalized people who weren't usually represented (or represented fairly) in the mainstream media that I consumed. This was a space where people got to represent themselves through their own gaze. For the first time I could seek out bisexual queer femmes living their best life, I listened to people of colour talk openly about their experiences with racism, and I learnt about the broad spectrum of sexuality and gender. It helped me unpack my fatphobia, thanks to the people who informed me of my bias in the way I only illustrated thin bodies. I learnt the importance of accountability through trained therapists on Instagram, and here I am today – *still learning*. I have utilized Instagram as a mirror, and the work of its creators has given me an in-depth reflection to better and more thoroughly understand myself. It's a space I have used to influence others and allowed others to influence me. If we want Instagram and social media to positively impact our lives and use it as a catalyst for growth, we must make a conscious effort to diversify and declutter our feeds.

REPROGRAM YOUR PATRIARCHAL BRAINWASHING

Your preferences are political. The way you view yourself and others is informed by the narratives and stereotypes you consume about those people through the media.

Social media gives us a chance to re-brainwash our disgusting racist, patriarchal and Western standards of beauty. A cracking example of a movement dedicated to revising our idea of beauty is Chidera Eggerue's hashtag #SaggyBoobsMatter, which has empowered people to cancel their surgery appointments for breast reduction/lifting. Another is #TransIsBeautiful which highlights the spectrum of trans identities and positions them in an empowering light, as opposed to the dehumanization and sexualization we see of them in the media. There are multitudes of pages dedicated to uplifting fat bodies, fashion blogs for physically disabled people, and queer couples just living their best lives. When mainstream media is overwhelmingly straight, cisgender, able-bodied and white, consuming this content is oxygen to me.

Search for empowering, educational, therapeutic Instagram accounts, and look for ones run by Black people, trans people and queer people on Google – there are so many articles and websites that highlight the best ones. Doesn't it sound nice to get lost in a social media hole that feels empowering, challenging and encourages inner growth, rather than sending you into a spiral of self-deprecation and comparison? These people will probably teach you more than you'll ever discover during your degree that you so readily rank up thousands in debt for – so remember to pay people for the education they give you where you can. Most people have links to their Paypal on their pages! Acknowledge how they have benefitted you and your education.

**Your happiness – the way you view yourself –
and the content you consume is in *your* control.
Make changes. Now.**

INSTANT GRATIFICATION IS A BOTTOMLESS PIT

However much I have gained and benefitted from utilizing Instagram as a platform, if left unchecked and un-moderated, its use can be detrimental to our mental health and self-image. If the foundation of our happiness and how we think about ourselves relies on the comments we receive from strangers on the internet, it is not real, lasting and fulfilling happiness. But we already knew that, because every time we upload content that doesn't get the usual amount of comments and likes, we're left feeling like a *pile of unvalidated shit.* Don't be fooled, this is all a very intentional effect of social media.

Sean Parker (the first president of Facebook) admitted that addiction is in fact not just a by-product of social media, *it's part of the design.* The unpredictability of social media is what makes it so addictive. Just like gambling, you never know what response you'll get when you post something – whether it's going to be positive or negative. Not knowing the outcome becomes a high, and each time we receive a positive response, our body releases endorphins to make us feel an overwhelming (but fleeting) sense of validation and excitement. The more frequently we engage with this algorithm, the more we learn to crave the next adrenaline rush.

Most of us are shackled to our devices. I know that my attention span and ability to focus on a task have reduced dramatically since using social media. I check my phone like clockwork even when it hasn't made a noise, I check my socials first thing in the morning and before I go to bed, I obsess over who has and hasn't liked my pictures and *what that means,* and I've projected my insecurities onto the comments that people have left on my posts, sending my mind into anxiety overdrive.

We all have a void that we're trying to fill, and social media assists in widening that void. Social media and the internet create a *dependency*.

It took me a while to notice the pattern, but when we are triggered by something or when we feel low, we try to fill that void – *quickly*. What our void really needs is tending to, it needs love and it needs to heal. *That void needs therapy.*

But with instant gratification becoming increasingly accessible, we find ourselves regularly settling for the quick fix. Artist Polly Nor shared a vulnerable illustration depicting a girl using her phone on the toilet, titled *She Only Swipes Right on Sundays*. After I saw this, I clocked that the only time I'd widened my search settings to include men on dating apps was on the Sundays that I was hungover, or at times when I was feeling insecure and I needed that *sweet hit* of male validation. I was twice as likely to swipe right and lower my standards when I was feeling low, and until that moment I didn't even know that this is what I was doing or that this was my pattern. I didn't even *want* to date these men! I never spoke to or met any of them. My void was screaming "FILL ME FLORENCE", and my subconscious knew that a quick way to do that was to grab my phone and be desired.

We indulge in a multitude of things to temporarily fill our void. But this void has been widened by our increasing access to instant gratification. We are living in a world where we can so readily be given immediate validation through comments on Instagram, casual sex through dating apps (when let's be real, what we're really craving is intimacy – *but we'll settle*)

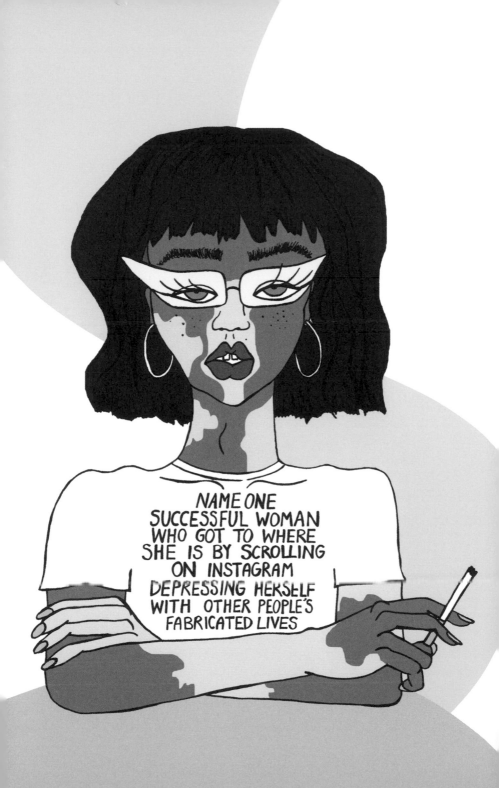

IT'S
NOT FAIR
ON YOUR MIND TO COMPARE
YOUR LOWEST MOMENTS
TO ANOTHER PERSON'S
HIGHLIGHT REEL,
ESPECIALLY
FIRST THING
IN THE
MORNING.

and food delivered to our door within minutes. We are living at peak content consumption, with a demand for instant services. Literally anything you want. You need an outfit for tomorrow night? You can have it delivered to your door the same day for a tenner. Craving a shag? *There's an app for that.* Need your make-up done for a last-minute event? Again, *there's an app for that!* You can order a masseuse, hair stylist or make-up artist (who's screened profile and background you can check in the app) to your door, within the hour.

The hunger to have things *now* is ever increasing, and so is the number of businesses available to keep up with this insatiable desire. It can be hard at times to allow ourselves to be slow in this world. Social media and the internet aren't going to disappear, but that's a good thing. Because if you can harness their power and make them work for you, they're bloody brilliant! But just like everything we engage with, we need to set and hold firm boundaries to be able to get what we want out of it. Here are a few that have worked for me and allowed me to get the best out of social media, and reduce some of the harmful effects it can have on mental health:

- Turn your phone off sometimes! Or if you can't turn it off, temporarily delete your social apps.
- Turn notifications on vibrate/loud so you're not tempted to keep frantically checking your phone like clockwork.
- Put your phone in your kitchen/living room before you go to bed, to stop the urge to scroll late at night and in the mornings. It's not fair on your mind to compare your lowest moments to another person's highlight reel, *especially* first thing in the morning.
- You are allowed to unfollow people. If they make you feel shit about yourself, unfollow them. Or, mute them. Work through why those feelings come up for you, and why this person makes you feel uncomfortable. Maybe it's nothing to do with them, maybe it's you. Different people evoke different emotions in us – acknowledge these

feelings and use this as a catalyst for growth, to understand more about yourself.

-   Follow accounts that encourage your growth and make you want to align with your highest self. Accounts that trash other women, promote an unhealthy dieting culture or are triggering for your mental health are going to keep you stagnant, suffering and stuck in old patterns.

-   Unapologetically block trolls and people who are harassing you. People on the internet do not get to dictate your happiness with spiteful projections of their insecurities. So often we can obsess over another person's comments and internalize something that's actually just a projection of their own insecurity. It's not about you. Don't take on someone else's problem.

-   If you have a community on Instagram, set boundaries with it. Take time to think about what you have energy for and tell your community what you will and won't be doing. This will also help you decide who to block, as people who don't respect your boundaries don't deserve access to your space. E.g. I don't give people advice when they ask for it in my DMs because 1. I'm not trained, 2. I'm not being paid to do that and 3. I don't work for free. I'm not a source of empowerment for people who have no intention of reciprocating that energy. *Emotional labour is still labour.*

PRESSURE TO PERFORM

If who you are changes and shifts depending on "what works well for the algorithm" and whichever palatable version of yourself you can showcase to generate a positive response – how long is it going to be before that version of yourself is what you feel shit about "not being able to live up to" in real life? We all compare ourselves to capitalist beauty standards, but it seems that with our highly curated lives on Instagram, we have created yet *another* standard we are constantly striving to achieve – the version of our life that we present online.

We put up the best bits of our lives on Instagram – the days our hair and make-up is looking good, when we're on our holidays, out with our friends, when we have had successes, going to parties and events. It's all a very surface-level presentation of what our lives actually look like because we are projecting the good moments to the world. A few things people don't see about my life are the therapy appointments I run home from crying, the mornings I struggle to get out of bed, the bins that still need taking out and the fact I haven't cooked myself a proper meal for over a month and have just been eating take-out in order to get work done. We are multifaceted human beings, and it's impossible to showcase *all* parts of ourselves to people at *all* times. The version we showcase to our followers makes up such a small percentage of who we are. But what do we actually "owe" our audience; do we owe them anything?

During the course of writing this book, I experienced the most traumatic and debilitating experience of my life – and my followers don't know anything about this. Only a handful of people I decided to choose – my friends and family in real life – knew about it. Why? Because I don't owe anyone my trauma. Social media can sometimes make it feel like we owe it to people to share with them the most intimate details of our lives in the name of "transparency" – but why cut yourself open and show the most vulnerable, unhealed and intimate parts of yourself if it feels uncomfortable? Opening up and being vulnerable should be reserved for times when it will benefit *your* healing – not for the sake of other people feeling entitled to know about your business. The view people have into my life is already incredibly intimate. People have seen the inside of my flat, they know who my friends are, what clothes I wear day-to-day, they know what makes me laugh...but all of this information is selective and curated. I show the parts of myself that I feel comfortable sharing, and these are some of the boundaries I have enforced to protect my energy.

It becomes problematic if left unchecked and unregulated, especially when people feel entitled to know what's going on in your life, and you start to believe that you owe it to them.

> **There is a compulsion to record, capture and showcase our moments of joy with the world on social media. But you deserve to keep some things for yourself.**

Not everyone deserves to know what fills you up. Some of the experiences in my life do not deserve to be laid out, vulnerable and cold, on the operating table for people to cut open. My trauma and experiences are mine, and they do not have to be dissected by thousands of people. I do not owe that to anyone. Neither do you.

"I AM NOT RESPONSIBLE FOR THE IDEA THAT YOU HAVE CREATED OF ME IN YOUR MIND"

If we're not careful, we can find ourselves using people on Instagram as screens for our projections and insecurities. The parts of our lives which we are lacking – we assume they have it in abundance. Although we only know about five per cent of their curated lives, still we project our own insecurities, shortcomings, fears, unhealed trauma and romanticized ideas about people to fill the gaps in what we know about them. Then, would you believe, we feel *entitled* to be disappointed when they don't turn out to be this person we made them out to be! I hate to break it to you, but people on Instagram don't owe you a *thing*. There's a certain amount of entitlement that we all have when it comes to the people we interact with and follow online. We want to know who they're dating. Who they're friends with. Where they like to go to eat. What places they frequent. We feel *entitled* to them as a resource of free consumable content, and we expect that content to be upheld to a certain level. We even hold them to levels of accountability that we do not even hold ourselves or the people in our lives to. We end up breaking our own hearts by expecting too much from people.

Learn to use the people you see online as a mirror, but also know that you are responsible for not projecting the parts of yourself you discover onto them. Sit in it instead.

You are never going to be your best if subconsciously you're trying to be *someone else's* best. Because you'll never be just like them – just like they'll never be just like you. In fact, are they even what you perceive as "them"? You're projecting your own ideas onto their Instagram feed, and that feed *itself* is curated, polished, and a highlight reel of five per cent of their life.

Name one person who is both happy and successful who got to where they are by obsessing over other people's fabricated lives on Instagram...

I'll wait.

CHAPTER 8

PROTECT YOUR ENERGY

First and foremost, your time and energy should be preserved above all for yourself. Anyone who wants to be a part of your life must be an addition to your wholeness. If you are subconsciously seeking someone to "make you whole", you're not ready for a relationship.

Sure, relationships can aid us in our journey of healing, and help us to accept parts of ourselves that we are yet to own fully and still feel insecure about. But if you put your worth and happiness *exclusively* into another person, the moment you part ways you'll be left with the same unhealed wounds you started off with, and now with an additional person-shaped void to fill too.

When we use other people to make us feel whole, we start to base our worth on how they treat us, and we can end up losing our self-worth and our sense of identity. Our worth should not be defined by how certain people treat us, and we cannot take it as a personal fault or a reflection of our worthiness when they project their *own* internalized suffering onto us by mistreating us. Prioritize the love you have for yourself so much that if a relationship ends, you aren't left feeling diminished. Because you already have a firm sense of who you are, and you realize that you are *more* than enough on your own.

People who focus on everyone but themselves tend to neglect their own needs in the process. Don't be tempted to buy into the heteronormative lie that wants women to exist for everyone but themselves – there's *nothing* noble about self-sacrifice.

Think about the person you could become if you stopped searching for value in your ability to fix others, and put that energy into yourself and your own life. Imagine the sheer power and confidence you would radiate! *Imagine.*

When you choose to focus on yourself, the things you once craved and the people from whom you once desperately needed validation will cease to become necessary. You realize you no longer need them. In fact, you never did. They were all temporary distractions from the real love of your life – yourself.

You don't have time in this life to be wasting precious energy on people who don't even realize what a privilege it is to know you. If they can't see how bloody fantastic you are, why would you want to be with them anyway? You can't expect *you* from people. Not everyone deserves to know you, and not everyone can reciprocate the energy that you are willing to pour into a relationship. Those people simply do not deserve to know you.

Move on.

To practise self-love and protect your energy, you need to start implementing boundaries with the people you surround yourself with. Remember: those who do not respect them do not deserve to know you.

Simple boundaries to start with include:

- Saying "no".
- Speaking up when someone is making you feel uncomfortable.
- If you need alone time, say so. You don't have to justify it.
- Delegating tasks, and saying "yes" to help from others.
- Stop apologizing if someone corrects you. Just say "thank you".

Questions to ask yourself daily as a way of checking in:

- Am I going to this event because I want to, or because I feel external pressure to?
- Do I have the capacity to help my friend out right now?
- Do I follow the advice I give to others?
- If I could give myself one thing this week, what would it be?
- What am I putting off right now?
- Do I feel comfortable in this moment?
- How do the people currently in my life make me feel?
- Have I been allowing myself to feel my feelings lately, or have I been minimizing them?
- Have I expressed to people how I'm feeling?
- Are people respecting my identity/identities?

SETTING BOUNDARIES

I constantly implement new boundaries as I learn more about my desires and what makes me uncomfortable, to ensure that people who do not seek to respect them no longer have the privilege of staying in my life. Verbally setting boundaries reveals to me who those people are, based on their response. Even though it's not my fault that these people are in my life, I have to hold myself accountable and remember that I have a part to play in how long I entertain them for. I have to

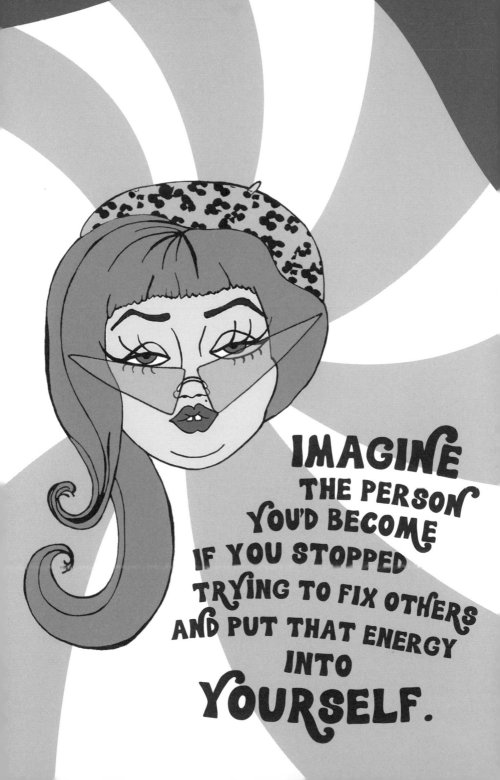

be honest with myself and admit that part of me still believes my worth is tied up in pleasing others, but learn that it isn't healthy to over-spend my energy while neglecting my own needs in the process. It's emotionally debilitating when people use you as a source for their own empowerment, and it's for this reason exactly that people pay money to go to therapy. Money is the reciprocal energy therapists are paid to make sure they are compensated for their professional advice and expertise. This is <u>not</u> a role you should be taking on with your friends or partners.

When I began setting boundaries and checking in with myself, I became aware of how I felt after spending time with certain people; it forced me to think about myself first and protect my energy.

My friends and I are obsessed with respecting each other and learning about one another's boundaries – and I don't think there's a love more important and beautiful than that.

WHAT BOUNDARIES DO YOU NEED TO PUT IN PLACE TO PROTECT YOUR OWN ENERGY?

Here are a few boundaries that will help you assess whether the people in your life respect you and deserve you.

Do you feel that you're able to say "no" to them?

"No" is the most definable, clear and communicative boundary, yet we often find ourselves feeling guilty for saying "no" to people, at the expense of our own comfort and desires. Agreeing to favours for friends every now and then and pushing yourself out of your comfort zone to experience something new and exciting is entirely different. That's what friends are for – growth! But it's a red flag when you feel like you might experience some form of guilt or punishment from this person for simply telling them "no". Punishment – aka using the fact you said "no" to get you to do things for them in the future, becoming passive-aggressive with silent treatment, cutting

off communication and ignoring your messages to make you feel
guilty – are all forms of emotional manipulation. These people are
bad news, and you should try to exit this relationship as soon as you can.
Work on healing the parts of yourself that thought you deserved this kind
of love in the first place. Inspect those wounds.

How does this person make you feel after seeing them?

If you're left feeling drained and depleted of energy, if their company
brings out a bad side in you or makes you agree to things you don't want to,
then they're waving a big old red flag right in your face. They're practically
smacking you in the face with it hun. Refuse to give the limited amount of
time you have in this life to people who bring out the worst version of you
and coerce you into doing things for their "approval", that you otherwise
would have never agreed to.

Does this person value your time?

Time is another important boundary and a real eye-opener when it comes
to how people value their relationship with you. If they always show up
late, cancel last minute, and only drop in your life when they need you,
they do not respect your time. This is not a reciprocal relationship. You
are being used for your energy! Don't give any time to people who don't
have time for you.

You do not owe anyone an explanation if you decide to distance yourself
from someone because they have violated your boundaries. However, if
you do decide to communicate to them that they have let you down and
not respected you as an attempt to preserve the friendship – and their
response focuses on excuses and how you "took it the wrong way" without
an apology, they're trying to make you doubt your very valid feelings.
This makes their behaviour "gaslighting". This is a form of emotional

manipulation, when someone purposefully leads you to think that you're the problem and that you're "too sensitive". You might even end up apologizing for taking their actions the wrong way.

GASLIGHTING

Gaslighting, when someone's lived experiences are deflected and made out to be in their head, is a form of emotional manipulation that often plays out in abusive relationships and can cause victims to lose their sense of self almost entirely. When people get defensive and say things like, "I didn't mean to, *you've* taken it the wrong way" or, "it was a joke", what this does is shift the blame onto the person who feels hurt, leaving them feeling responsible for dealing with their feelings and often causing them to question their own reality. Here are some examples:

Straight up lying

Say you saw the person you're dating kiss someone else in a bar, you confront them about it the next morning and they tell you they were in all evening watching TV and that you must be "going mad". This is a form of manipulative gaslighting, making you believe it's all in your head.

Denial

They say something to you and when you bring it up at a later date, they deny ever saying it without leaving the slightest room for possibility that they might have just forgotten. "Nope, I never said that. That's in your head. Why would I say that to you?" If it gets to the point where you feel like you actually need to record conversations with someone, run. Really. If they have you doubting yourself this much, you're more than likely dealing with a narcissist. Get the hell outta there!

Denial of your lived experiences

Let's say a Black man is recalling a time he was stopped and searched on his way into a nightclub, but none of the white guys were. He's confiding in his white friend about this experience, and his friend turns around and says, "Not everything's about race, don't play that card. It was probably a random check." This is a form of gaslighting, making him question if it really is all in his head.

Calling you "crazy"

Their aim with this word is to manipulate you to the point of doubting your own reality *so much*, that you merge with their reality instead. They may also call you "crazy" to other people so that if you were ever to seek help from others, they would have already built a solid case that you're too "psycho" or "crazy" to be trusted. They have a better chance of keeping you manipulated if they can isolate you and make sure that no one believes you. An example of how gaslighting is used as a tactic to perpetuate racism on a global scale, is how when Black women express themselves and are vocal about their oppression, whether on the news or in real life, they are often dismissed (or intentionally portrayed) as *"just another angry/ aggressive Black woman"*. We see their anger as an "over reaction", but never question where that anger came from in the first place – we don't examine the roots of their anger, because we have already been trained through racist stereotypes in the media not to trust, listen to or believe Black women. As a result, their valid anger and expression is unfairly dismissed (this perspective was brought to my attention by the work of Rachel Ricketts).

BE SMART WITH YOUR ENERGY. TREAT IT LIKE THE CURRENCY OF YOUR BUSINESS.

Check in with yourself and others regularly to encourage the preservation of energy in your friendship groups. Help each other to prioritize and preserve your resources. Resources could be anything from time or energy, to money. Whatever it is, whatever form it takes, big or small – put yourself first.

Your energy is a limited currency. If you're spending too much doing things for other people and spreading yourself too thin, let your friends know that you simply don't have the capacity to meet them this week. Check in with yourself regularly to see how much energy you have left in your bank, as if it were your savings. Keep an eye on your income and outgoing expenses – how much you give to others, and how much you receive yourself. You cannot run on empty, the same way a business cannot be profitable if it doesn't receive more money than it is spending. Before over-extending yourself in a situation, ask yourself if it's even necessary.

Women are constantly expected to be "nice". What that really means is "perform emotional labour for free". If you don't conform? You're a *bitch*. When people call me a "bitch" or say that I'm "intimidating", all I hear is the sound of their own insecurities and lack of self-worth, because I used to be that person! The doormat, being walked over by everyone in my life, calling others who set boundaries – a *bitch*. But setting boundaries protects you from compromising yourself. It may initially make you feel guilty, but delegating your energy without worrying about how others see you is an essential survival technique that women have been discouraged from using.

Respect yourself and your energy better than freely giving it to people who have no intention of reciprocating. Don't devalue it like that.

Stop saying "sure" to everything when really you mean "no".

If protecting your energy and refusing to entertain things that don't nourish your soul makes you a "bitch" – then go ahead, be a bitch.

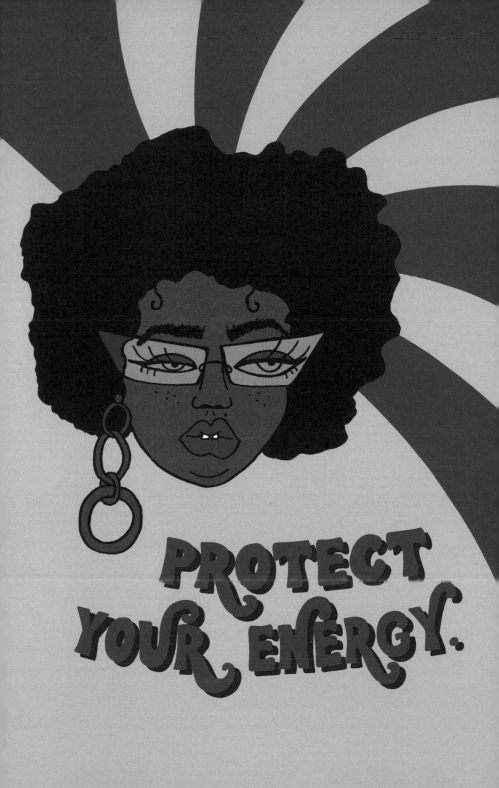

CHAPTER 9

TO DATE OR NOT TO DATE

There is so much power in knowing what you do and don't want from life, and dating someone new is an opportunity for you to practise setting your boundaries and protecting your energy. Going on dates, whether they turn out well or not, offers endless possibilities to learn about all the different sides of yourself.

Before going on a first date with someone, you must remember that human beings are multifaceted. During the date, they will only be shining a light on the most attractive facets of themselves and presenting their best bits. There's a whole other side of them you know nothing about, full of history, past relationships, behaviours and trauma. Which means if you fall in love with someone at first sight it's not the *person* you're falling for. You're falling for your projection and romanticized idea of them, as you don't know all of their "stuff". "Falling in love at first sight" isn't romantic, it's actually a sign of unhealthy boundaries.

This is why looking out for red flags on the first date is crucial. View a first date like an interview – you're both trying to see if you could work well together. That's not to say you should barrage your date with intimidating questions, but it's important to keep in mind that you're not the only one here who has to make a good impression. Would you interrupt someone in an interview to use your phone? Would you show up late to an interview? Would you *hire* someone who was late to an interview? If they're already exhibiting toxic patterns of behaviour, oversharing, or checking their phone constantly – what are they going to be like when they're *comfortable*?

Are you one of those people who has been going about their life saying they're fed up with attracting the same time-wasters and assholes? I *hate* to be the one to break it to you hun, but if there's a pattern, part of that will be down to your low self-esteem because we accept the love we think we deserve. It's hard to do – but part of growing is acknowledging the uncomfortable truth that although we did not deserve whatever treatment we received, abuse in our society is normalized. When something is normalized, we accept it and it remains unchallenged. We settle for mediocre partners because we don't believe we deserve better, or believe that "better" even existed for "someone like us". If left unchecked, we can end up subconsciously seeking partners who require the care and attention that really we wish we could give to ourselves. This is a form of projecting, avoiding the healing that we need to do ourselves by distracting ourselves with wanting to fix others. Your willingness and urge to fix everyone and direct that energy away from yourself is a sign you have wounds to heal that you're ignoring. Go tend to them.

> **"When someone shows you who they are,**
> **believe them the first time." – Maya Angelou**

They might be hot, but if they're a piece of shit – *they're a piece of shit.* Learn to let go of people at the first sight of a red flag, before you even *contemplate* compromising yourself and your standards for them. Demanding better for yourself and your life is

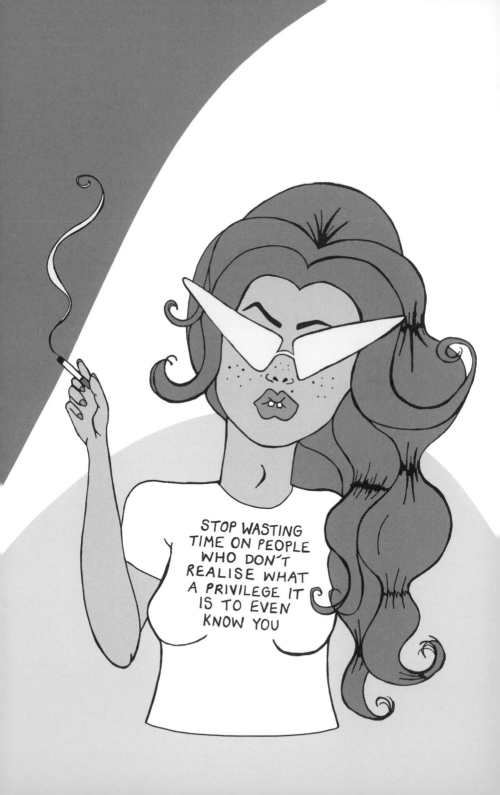

hard, especially because at times it *will* be lonely. But whenever you're tempted to settle remember: you date someone's emotional maturity. Not their *jawline.* Ignoring your red flags or "deal breakers" will be the reason things don't work out in the long run anyway.

We're not settling for crumbs, ever.

Remember?

I once went on a first date with a man who was in therapy, good looking, and had a thriving career – in short, it was going very well. That was until he brought up his ex and said he "can't date girls who spend too much time on their looks anymore". He followed this up by saying he doesn't believe in the wage gap. *You can only imagine the look on my face.* I told him right there and then that I didn't think we'd be compatible due to our different views, thanked him for the drink, and ordered my ride home. No time wasted trying to fix him. No wishful thinking that I could help "grow this man" into an open-minded feminist – *I'm not looking for a project.* You cannot fall in love with someone's "potential" hun. You're just kidding yourself. It's a form of projection because you're falling for a version of them that *doesn't exist,* and filling in the gaps of their character with what you want and need from them. But you can't change people. He showed me who he was, and I chose to love myself enough to believe him *the first time.*

Stop asking yourself if you're good enough for people. Are they even good enough for *you?*

We can get so wrapped up in how we are perceived by others on a date that we don't pay nearly enough attention to whether or not we even like them, or whether their attention is just propping up our ego, making us feel wanted. Don't get the two mixed up. It can be especially hard if you're not used to people paying attention to you, but this rule applies to everyone – we *all* deserve to be respected in the ways that we desire. We often project on our dates the romanticized ideas and heteronormative aspirations we have been schooled in since we were young, and, as Wanda says in *BoJackHorseman*, "when you look at someone through rose-tinted glasses, all the red flags just look like flags".

Stay vigilant.

QUEER FIRST DATES

Queer first dates don't have a script and there are fewer gender roles at play, but a lot of my queer dates are hilariously formulaic. They usually involve chatting shit about capitalism, finding out you've dated the same person, telling your coming-out story, talking for hours as you slowly edge closer to each other because no one wants to make the first move...it's beautiful. I love the experience of being able to be my fully blossomed self and not feeling the need to fulfill a prescribed gender role. The only issue is that often I find myself sat there wondering the entire time...

"Is this a date or are we just hanging out?"

I wish someone had warned me how ambiguous queer dating can be. Not only do you have to find out if they're single, but you need to find out if they're even queer (which usually involves relentlessly scrolling through their Instagram page to find some form of a rainbow flag). And then you have to find out if they're into you – or if they just want to be your friend.

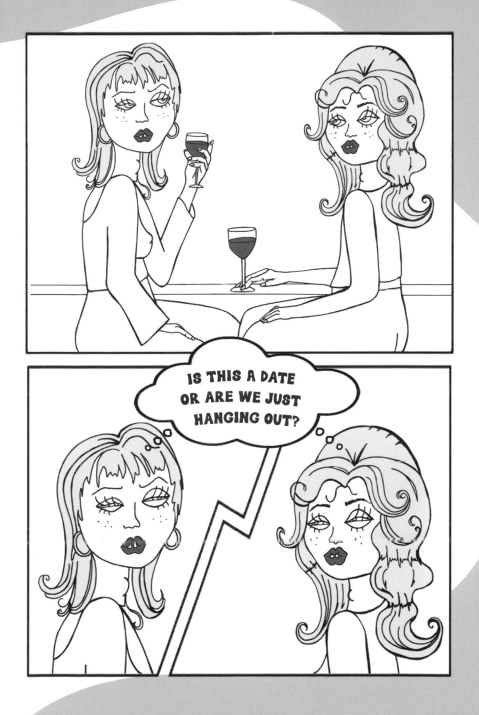

With the amount of ambiguous "maybe dates" I've been on with women, I can tell you that it isn't worth the mental or physical energy "waiting to find out on the date". Don't do it to yourself, you both need and deserve clarity. As there's no prescribed narrative for us to relate to, queer dating can be a bit of a long game – but *it doesn't have to be.* You're going to need to sharpen up on your communication skills if you want to navigate the queer dating scene (and not be confused the whole time). *Especially* if you're a femme! The world assumes that you're straight because of the way you express your gender, and straight girls who "wanna go for a drink" don't realize how confusing that sentiment is to someone who wants to go for a drink...*and maybe back to your place afterwards.* Spare yourself the energy and communicate your desires directly, babe.

"Do you want to go for a drink?" isn't clear enough when it comes to dating other queer people, especially if they have no clue you're also queer. If you're unsure, you're going to need to pointedly ask them if they'd like to go on a date with you. Or if they ask you – you're going to have to ask *them* if it's a date. The worst thing that could happen is that they say they're not queer, available or interested! Asking people up-front has strengthened my confidence and my ability to handle rejection. I'd much rather find out that someone is straight or simply not interested from the beginning and have a chat with my ego about that hit of rejection in my own time, than go on a "maybe date", spending the whole time analysing their body language, waiting for them to make a move and going home even *more* confused than I was before. Being honest about what you want, and communicating it, is sexy as hell. It also makes life a lot more straight forward.

Protect your energy. *Ask them if it's a date.*

WHEN TO DATE

> "I no longer date when I'm vibrating at a low frequency.
> It's like placing myself on a clearance rack." – Necole Kane

Crumbs are only tempting when you're hungry, so you must ensure that you're always full on your own. Avoid seeking out dates when you're feeling low or processing recent break-ups – that's when you enter "settling for less than you deserve" territory, repeat cycles of self-destructive behaviour, and end up dating people who simply *don't* deserve to know you. In the past I've dated and entertained people who weren't good enough for me purely because I wasn't feeling good about myself. I just wanted someone to *see me*. But the best way to get over someone is *not* to "get under" someone else. They will distract you temporarily, sure. But by doing this you're just measuring your self-worth based on your love life again, and seeking validation in others to prove to yourself that you're worthy. If you're not in a particularly stable place and you're feeling low, or you're at a place in your life where you're craving external validation, it can be very easy to get swept up in someone's allure and ignore red flags or controlling behaviours. When you're low, if you're not vigilant with how you spend your energy, you're more likely to allow the first person that makes you feel special and whole again to enter your life, whether they're good for you or not. This is where toxic relationships flourish.

You are in a far better position to date when you love yourself, because:
- You start to see your worth outside of being coupled with someone else's shared identity.
- You start to realize your worth as a unique and individual whole person, as opposed to someone else's "other half".

- You'll abstain from your need to settle, because you don't need someone to complete you. *You complete you.*
- You're more in touch with your needs and desires, so saying "no" to people who don't match your standards won't feel hard. It will feel like self-care. It will feel invigorating.

Add value to my life, or bust.

I'm extra as hell with how I spend my energy, and I don't care what anyone thinks of that. I've had to get on my hands and knees to scrape my life back together after it has been shattered to pieces by people far too many times to just allow any person to wander into my space again. When it comes to my life, there's no way I'm living it unchecked and without making sure I'm doing what's best for me. My boundaries are non-negotiable.

After I once had a debilitating dating experience, I wrote up something I call "The Checklist", to ensure that I never compromise my standards and boundaries when it comes to someone new entering my life ever again. This way, no matter if I'm feeling low or doubtful of myself, I can look at the list and be reminded that I should never have to settle. My checklist keeps me accountable.

These are a few things on my checklist:
- Does this person challenge me in a healthy way?
- Have they demonstrated that they respect my time?
- Are they a feminist?

I also have a list of red flags, including:

- Do they say things to me that I'd feel uncomfortable repeating to a friend?
- Do they only talk about themselves?
- Do they talk negatively of others, for no reason?

...you get the picture.

So, go write your version of "The Checklist". Of course, your list will look a *lot* different to mine. Do not try to apply the same standards as me if they don't work for you, or if they're not as important to you. This is just my personal way to check in with myself, ensuring that I'm always receiving the treatment I want and deserve. Regardless of where I'm at with my self-esteem, I always deserve the best.

YOUR DATING "PREFERENCES" *ARE* POLITICAL

"I don't date feminine guys."

"I have a thing for Asian girls."

"I don't like girls who are high maintenance."

"I like girls who can be one of the guys."

"I can't stand drama."

"I've only dated Black guys."

We all have preferences when it comes to dating people, whether it's preferences for their tastes, interests or career prospects. But when it comes to someone's identity our preferences when dating are inherently political – just as they are when it comes to hiring. The difference is that when it comes to hiring, there are systems in place that make it illegal to discriminate, ensuring that people of colour, queer folks and marginalized people are hired, or at the very least not discriminated against in the hiring process. If a company is found unfairly discriminating it can be held to account. So when it comes to dating, how have we convinced ourselves that our "preferences" aren't influenced by our unconscious biases of prejudice and racism, just as they are in the work place? Most people assume we all have different tastes and *that's just it*. But what informs our taste?

(Hint: it's "desirability politics".)

When it comes to who we date and who we find attractive, our collective "preferences" as a society are informed by our subconscious bias, our cultural influences, and who we are *taught to find attractive* through the media and the narratives we consume about the hierarchy of beauty. Which makes every single person's desire and desirability inherently political.

Do you listen to and respect people you're not attracted to?

I sit high on the scale of desirability, being slim, non-disabled, white, cisgender and feminine. People open up to me and see me as "nice" and "innocent" before I even get a chance to open my mouth. I could be *awful* but I am afforded many privileges as a result of being "desired" by society. Because I am white, I am more likely to be seen and heard. Because my gender expression aligns with society's expectations, I am more likely to be desired. Because I am thin, I have the luxury of being able to dress myself in whatever clothes I like, I don't have to worry about stores not having my size, and I am not questioned about my health choices. Because I am cisgender, people don't question me about my genitals when shopping for clothes the same way they might a trans person. *By existing in the body that I do, I am treated better by society – and that isn't fair.*

It is important to acknowledge that some people are afforded *unearned* privileges for looking more "desirable" than others. And that while desirability is subject to our individual tastes, society's *collective* idea of

BEING HONEST ABOUT WHAT YOU WANT AND COMMUNICATING IT IS SEXY AS HELL.

beauty is informed and controlled by the same racist, fatphobic and sexist beauty standards, and there *is* a hierarchy. Our racist, homophobic, fatphobic society prioritizes people who conform to the narrative, and these people receive better treatment just for existing in the body they do.

DON'T CONFLATE "RESPECT" WITH FETISHIZATION

As you learn to reconnect with the humanity that has been bashed out of your brain since you were younger (no, this isn't going to be a comfortable process), remember not to confuse *respecting* marginalized people with *fetishizing* them.

A lot of white people, for example, think that if their dating history consists exclusively of Black people, their dating preferences aren't racist. But fetishization is as much a problem as avoiding dating certain people. When we fetishize marginalized people – whether fat, trans, PoC or disabled – we rid them of their chance to be the unique, multifaceted individual that they are. Saying, "I have a thing for Asian girls" – however well-intentioned – isn't a compliment, you're assuming that you know everything about them. They do not all act as one homogenous group. You'll find that the people who say this will rarely date the folks who don't fit into the stereotype either. Are they dating *all types* of Asian girls, or just the ones who match the stereotypes they have consumed? It doesn't matter if a stereotype about a particular group of people is "positive", the amount of pressure marginalized people feel when they have to live up to these stereotypes is unfair and harmful.

If we want to take back the control from our subconscious while we navigate the dating world — and shake up the unequal hierarchy that is desirability which exists in all communities, including LGBTQ+, we have to start by questioning our preferences.

Each time I date someone new it's an opportunity to learn about myself, as well as this other person. When I download dating apps I analyse each profile before I swipe left and ask myself, "*Why* am I not attracted to this person?" It sounds extra, but doing this has helped me to unpack and work through a lot of my unconscious bias that I didn't realize I had, rather than just accepting that "they're not my type". If you get just *one* take away from this book, I want it to be the action of questioning everything. *Including yourself.*

THIS WAY TO THE SHRINKING MACHINE...

In my experience, a lot of my interactions with cis men make me feel like I'm being placed into a shrinking machine. A machine designed to make me just the right amount of desirable, but not *too* sexy and not *too* eye-catching, so as not to give him the "wrong idea". Just the right amount of interesting, but not *too* interesting and not *too* intelligent, so as not to make him feel emasculated or uncomfortable. In fear of challenging the status quo that says *he's* supposed to be the confident one, I find myself constantly treading on eggshells, to avoid expressing myself in a way that might "emasculate him" or damage his ego. It's a pretty exhausting performance and one that women have been doing for centuries. Until we have fully rinsed out the conditioning that women need to shrink themselves around men to accommodate their "masculinity" and take up as little space as possible, we will forever be compromising our multifaceted selves for the sake of their egos.

When I "came out" as queer there was an uncomfortable transition I had to undergo, forcibly stepping outside this shrinking machine (dating cis men), so that I could allow myself the freedom to behave outside of society's archaic gender roles on dates. I wasn't used to living and dating in an uncompromised and unapologetic space. Suddenly dating people who were more likely to respect my boundaries and didn't expect me to be "smaller" felt initially like rejection, as I had learned to associate love with constant "compromise" and the need to lower my standards.

If you've been in the shrinking machine for a while, dating people without performing gender roles, without adhering to heteronormative standards, without allowing toxic behaviour and being expected to make yourself smaller can feel uncomfortable. It forces you to see that you always deserved better, and that you have lived a life of settling and shrinking. But try to view this discomfort as a growing pain that you have to endure, and find coping mechanisms to push on through. *This is good for you.* Whether you're transitioning into dating people of different genders or not, any healthy relationship after a toxic one, regardless of gender, can seem quiet and dull when you're used to chaos and danger. Just try to remember that this is healthy and that you deserve consistency and communication. You deserve this room to breathe and be your multifaceted self.

When you date emotionally unavailable people, some might say you even become *addicted* to the suffering. The unpredictability of dating them can in fact psychologically be what drives us to want more of it. It is the human condition to want something more when we don't know the outcome, whether or not we might "win". Just like gambling. Our mood hormones serotonin, dopamine and norepinephrine actually cause us to behave like addicts who want more and more, and our hearts actually accelerate faster when people ghost us and drop in and out of our lives.

How tragic.

We are *wired* to fall in love with emotionally unavailable people.

GHOSTING

> "Remember that not getting what you want is sometimes
> a wonderful stroke of luck" – Dalai Lama

Being ghosted can be one of the most challenging things to overcome when you start dating, because when you're left with no explanation of why these wounds have been inflicted, you reflect this inwards. You internalize it, and you see it as a personal fault.

Let's say you had an incredible night with someone who said they'd love to see you again, but they never followed through and didn't text you back. There are a multitude of reasons someone might ghost you – but none of them are about you. *Remember what I said about short-term validation?* (see page 41). If you've been ghosted, it's likely that you're the victim of a person who was experiencing low self-worth which led to them interacting with you as a means of instant gratification. It's likely *you* were their dopamine "hit" to temporarily fill their empty void. (*Ouch*, I know. I'm sorry.) But remember, the way people treat you is only ever a reflection of how they feel about themselves, not you. What people don't seem to realize, because of the normalization of ghosting, is how emotionally abusive it is to repeat this cycle of violence, especially when the ghost doesn't just stay away – they continue to drop in and out of your life, feeding you crumbs. Their absence causes you to question your self-worth, wondering what you "did wrong" to deserve this. This self-doubt makes it much easier for them to drop back in whenever they're bored and they want you, as they have planted this seed of craving inside you that needs their validation to alleviate these feelings of low self-worth, *that they are responsible for creating!* They created the void, the supply *and* the demand. It actually works a little bit like capitalism.

Ghosting should not be a normalized and widely accepted part of dating as it often manifests itself in these subtle forms of emotional abuse.

> **My advice to someone who has been ghosted?**
> ***Move on.* Do not prolong your suffering. They**
> **don't like you.**

Don't waste any more energy even thinking about this person. No more going over the details with your friends, grasping at straws trying to make excuses for them, or checking up on their socials and wondering if they ever think about you. If someone likes you, they will make it known. Stop wasting your limited time on this planet – time that could be spent working on yourself – wallowing around in "what if?" They're certainly not spending any of their energy thinking about *you*. They have chosen not to communicate with you and they didn't close the door, so you're going to have to close it yourself. You deserve consistency and communication – why in the name of hell would you settle for less? Unrequited love's a bore. We needn't accept crumbs of validation from unworthy people anymore. We want and *deserve* the whole damn cake.

DO YOU EVEN WANT TO SEE THIS PERSON AGAIN, OR CAN YOUR EGO JUST NOT HANDLE BEING UNWANTED?

Task: If you don't do it already, I want you to practise giving the closure and communication you expect to receive from others to the people that you are no longer keen on. There will be a few instances where you need to go no-contact on someone to protect your safety, but outside of that there is almost no reason to avoid communication. Whether that's letting your hairdresser know that you're cancelling an appointment so they can book other clients, letting the people you're dating know that you're only looking for something casual, texting a one-night stand to let them know that's as far as you'd like it to go, or communicating to your partner when you feel disrespected instead of becoming passive-aggressive in the hope they "figure it out". So many unpleasant interactions can be avoided by just employing direct communication.

People respect people who respect their time – it goes both ways.

Let's close the communication gap.

CHAPTER 10

MAYBE IT'S A GIRL CRUSH, MAYBE YOU'RE QUEER

Your queer feelings are entirely valid.

Let me start with a bit of clarification, as the words we use and the way we use them matter. It's important to know that the word "queer" has its roots in the history of queer *oppression,* not empowerment. It originally came into use in the 16th century and meant "strange" or "odd", then began to be used as an insult in the early 19th century towards people who were believed to be in same-sex relationships. However, LGBTQ+ activists in the 1980s reclaimed the word "queer" as a political statement to self-describe their identity.

Today, "queer" is widely used as a term for sexual orientation and gender identities that are not heterosexual or cisgender. If you're not straight, or you don't identify with the same gender you were assigned at birth, you may wish to self-identify as queer. Queer covers all sorts of sexual/gender identities, such as bisexual, asexual, non-binary and gender-fluid. It's important to remember that queerness is political.

Equally, some people still remember times when "queer" was used as a slur against them and because of this they don't feel comfortable adopting this label – which is valid too.

Rigid and archaic gender roles got in the way of living my truth for so long. Any time I vocalized my feelings for women and other genders as a closeted bisexual, I was often told that these feelings were just a "fantasy", and a fantasy only to be carried out for the entertainment of men. On top of this there was a lot of internalized homophobia to work through, which for me sounded in my head like, "You don't look queer enough" or "You've never been with a woman, how do you even know?" But I did know.

I knew because at times I'd had to think about women during sex.

I knew because I had fallen in love with my female friends.

I knew because my thoughts about women were recurring, and the thought of being in a relationship with a woman made me feel at home with myself.

I had always been compelled towards women – but I was *also* attracted to men and people of other genders. So what was it that stopped me from owning my queerness?

One night after consuming a lot of cocktails I ended up crying to my best friend, confessing my feelings for women, and that this was a whole part of my identity that I felt I hadn't given air to (I'm very dramatic). I was in a toxic long-term relationship with a man at the time, and I hadn't allowed the queer in me to breathe. As a femme, I never saw another person who looked like me dating girls in the media or in real life, and I thought that people who felt the way I felt *and* looked the way I looked, didn't exist. My limited, stereotypical understanding of queerness stopped me from validating my feelings. It's even harder for marginalized people (Black queer people, disabled queer people etc) to come to terms with their sexuality, as they're less likely to see themselves represented in the media at all, let alone *also* represented as queer. But the way you express yourself, how you dress and your other intersecting identities have no direct correlation with your sexuality. I learned to see these things as they exist individually, and outside of the binary. Who says queer *doesn't* look me? Why can't I date women and *also* have a feminine gender expression? I realized that by invalidating my own queerness, I was stereotyping other queer people. There is no one way to look, present or act queer. If you are queer, then you look queer.

The stereotypes about the gay community and how being queer is "supposed to look" (i.e. a traditionally masculine gender expression, short hair) stopped me from embracing an enormous part of my identity, and a lot of this has to do with an oversaturation of heteronormativity (encouragement of heterosexuality and gender roles), and therefore *lack* of queer representation in the media and public domain. My understanding of bisexuality was simple – it didn't exist. I never forget a friend once telling me, "My dad says bisexuals don't exist. You'll never meet a woman over 30 who still identifies as bisexual, it's a phase." As a teenager who was having an internal battle between my multifaceted self, and what the world, my peers and family expected of me as a young woman – I internalized this message, shamed away my feelings for women, put them into a box in my head and labelled it "Girl Crushes". The term "Girl Crush" was really just my creative way of saying "no homo". I was deeply embarrassed to admit my feelings for women.

If you're one of those people who talks of having girl crushes or says to their friends, "If I was gay I'd totally date her", have you ever considered that sexuality exists on a spectrum, and that you don't have to be "one or the other"? If you say you'd like to date her, maybe it means you actually just *want to date her*?! Bisexuality/pansexuality by definition means "attraction to more than one gender"; if you are attracted to other genders as well – this doesn't take away your attraction to men! I decided in my late

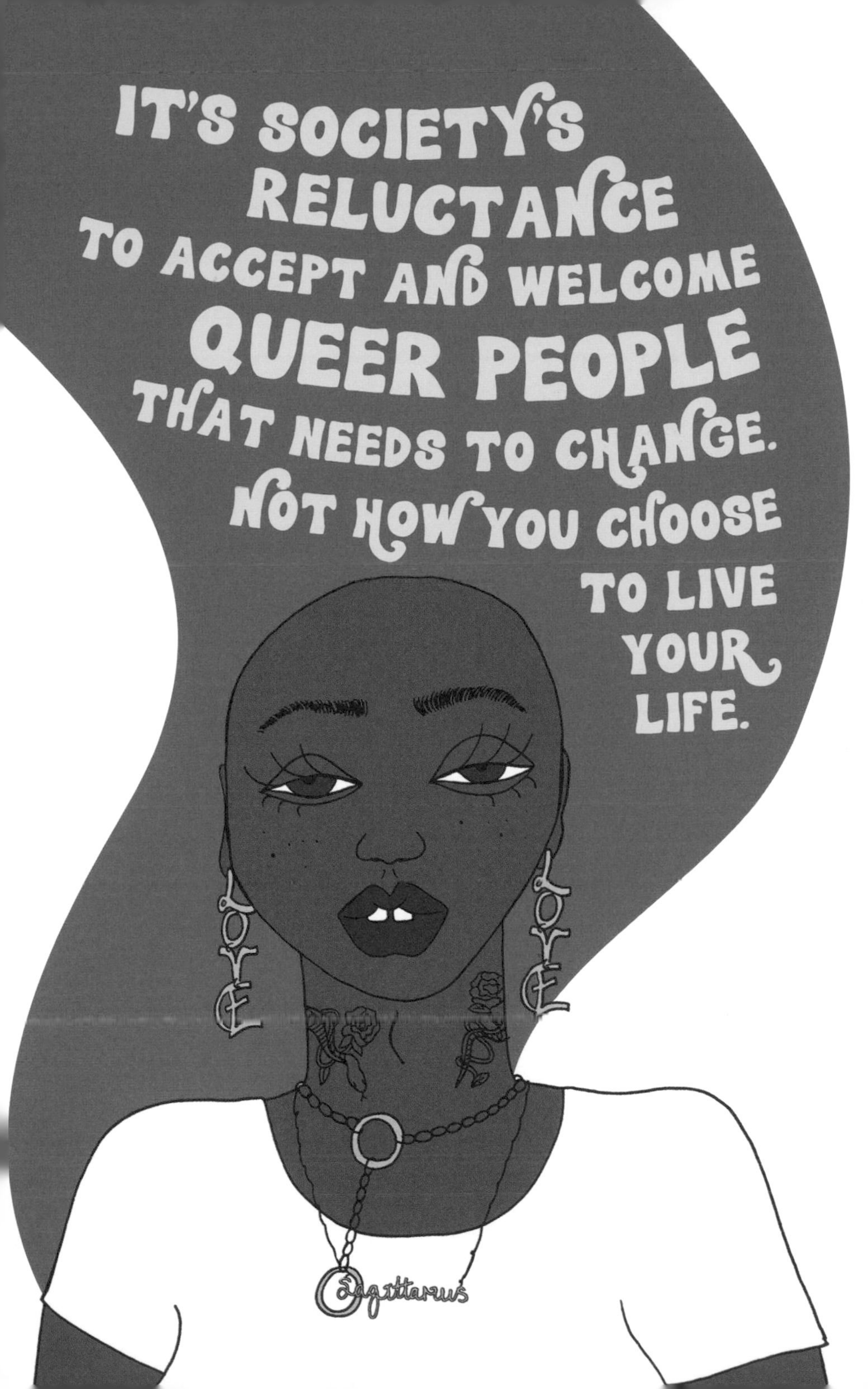
IT'S SOCIETY'S RELUCTANCE TO ACCEPT AND WELCOME QUEER PEOPLE THAT NEEDS TO CHANGE. NOT HOW YOU CHOOSE TO LIVE YOUR LIFE.
LOVE
LOVE

teens to unpack the "Girl Crush" box of shame in my head and address that these were just genuine crushes I had on other human beings.

The shame that women have surrounding sex is the same shame that seeps into our desire to be with other genders, because we are taught that our bodies exist and belong to the male gaze — so having feelings for other women is bound to confuse us.

For most women for our entire lives it has been imprinted, stamped, engraved and carved into our brains that one day we will marry a man and have his children. Dating and falling in love with a woman goes against this narrative. *How dare we be with anyone but a cis man?*

Heterosexuality is the fairy tale we are spoon-fed growing up. We see it on our TV screens, learn about it in sex-ed and read about it in our bedtime stories. I like to call this relentless bombardment, quite simply, *hetrifying*. Something so straight and heteronormative, that it makes you feel *hetrified*. There's a lot of debate about casting "too many" queer roles in the media in fear that it will brainwash the youth. But queer representation in the media isn't going to brainwash your child, boomer. Because heteronormativity *already has*.

There's a hierarchy of how relationships are viewed in our society, and ones that are comprised of cisgender, white, non-disabled, heterosexual, middle-class, married people with kids are placed on top. But here's the beautiful thing about being queer – by just existing outside of these definitions you get to throw society's restrictive rulebook out of the window. You get to write your own damn script and you can freestyle, as there is far less pressure to adhere to any previous ideas of romance, sex and "relationship progression".

THE FEMALE GAZE

"The influence of heteronormativity and the male gaze was so strong that I, someone who has fallen intensely in love with multiple women, felt like an imposter calling myself bisexual." – Ramona Marquez

As a bisexual woman, I questioned why it is that I don't enjoy viewing women in the same way that men do. Why I don't get instantly turned on from looking at hyper-sexualized images of women, and why it doesn't arouse me. I realized that it's because portraying women in this light wasn't created to suit my sexual needs. It wasn't created to satiate my queer sexual desires. Women are positioned as sexual objects of desire in the media to feed the appetite of the *male* gaze (see page 150).

When the dominant narrative of our society is heteronormative, I doubted my bisexuality because the only way I'd ever been taught that you can love women was to sexualize them. Which is far from the truth – healthy relationships are *not* built on objectifying or fetishizing your partner but on respecting them and seeing them as full human beings, not sexual ornaments.

The sexualization of women's bodies is so normalized, it made me question whether loving a woman outside of her objectification was valid enough. That if I didn't objectify women and talk about them the way cis men did, that I couldn't possibly be queer. *How hetrifying*.

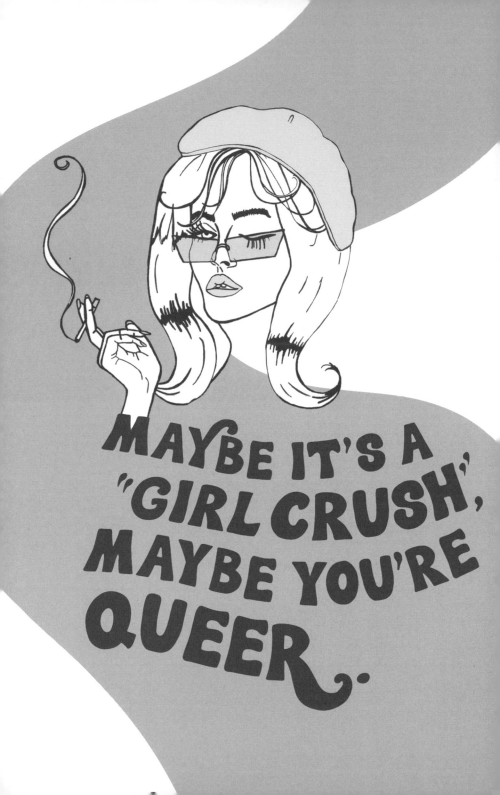

Despite my desire to date, have sex and be in relationships with women and non-binary people, I just didn't look at them in the same way that cis men did. I didn't see pictures of naked women and react in the same way that men did. I saw *myself* in them, I saw a multifaceted human being.

The idea of going to a strip club or gawking at a woman in a night club didn't elicit the same response from me as it did from my male counterparts. For some queer women it will, and that's also valid! But I didn't have the language to describe the capacity in which I felt I was attracted to women, because it wasn't in the way men typically did. But the reason most queer people don't instantly view women in a sexual way is because we're not viewing them through the lens of the heterosexual male gaze. We're not holding their beauty to the same standards. We look at them instead through our own gaze – the queer gaze.

Give yourself room to work through your desires and what influences them – what is it about the people you're attracted to that makes you like them? Whether you identify as part of the LGBTQ+ community or not, here are some questions you can use to reflect on your own life, and what role heteronormativity has played in your identity:

- In what ways has heteronormativity had an effect on your life?
  In what ways have the unwritten rules of how your gender "should behave" affected your everyday life, your body language, who you date, your self-expression and sex life?
- Do you assume people's sexuality or gender just by looking at them?
- Have you shamed away *your* queer feelings?

CHAPTER 11

LOVE SEX, HATE SEXISM

... AND *NEVER* FAKE AN ORGASM

It takes two to tango, so why is a woman's pleasure in heterosexual relationships still so rarely prioritized?

Why are we shamed for even implying that we enjoy sex, that we are able to take pleasure into our own hands through masturbation, and have multiple sexual partners the same way cis het men do? What kind of a message does it send to young women if we teach them that only men are supposed to enjoy sex? Are we just supposed to be a mere counterpart to their orgasm? Where does *our* pleasure fit into this? When our sex education is saturated with heteronormativity and lacking in discussion surrounding consent, it's not surprising that so many people are subject to unnecessary trauma during their first time. *Because not one of us knows what the fuck we're doing.*

Sex positivity is about bodily autonomy and your intrinsic right to express your sexuality however you desire. Whether that's by learning what you like and practising on yourself, meeting someone on Tinder for a commitment-free hook up, or deciding that sex isn't a priority for you at all because you've discovered that you're on the asexual spectrum – all of these are ways of expressing your sexuality. Because guess what? There *is* no norm.

Everything in life is experienced on a spectrum, everything you feel is valid and exists. It's also allowed to *fluctuate* up and down, depending on where you are in life and what you need at that stage. You need only to listen to yourself and your needs in order to discover what sex means for you, and what that looks like. Just make sure that you're doing what feels right for you.

LEARN TO FUCK YOURSELF

I found out how to make myself orgasm from a very young age, and it takes me *seconds* now. I remember worrying that I'd walk downstairs afterwards and there would be a mark on my face, some kind of "universally acknowledged indicator" that would reveal what I had been up to, and my parents would find out. The guilt was actually so unbearable I once dramatically burst into my mum's room to confess to her that I had "tingly feelings" watching the scene with Rizzo and Kenickie getting it on in the car in *Grease*. The reason I'm sharing my discovery of masturbation with you is because I want to destigmatize it. I can't even count the amount of times I heard (and believed) that "girls don't like sex" as I was growing up. You hear something repeated enough times, it starts to feel like the truth. When we are taught we "don't like sex", all that teaches us about our sexuality and our bodies is that they are to be reserved exclusively for men, and *their* sexual desires. It normalizes us as "passive participants" in sex, and not people who enjoy the experience equally. This narrative is particularly harmful for queer women and often prevents them coming out until later in life. A lot of queer women have sex with men because the normalization of discomfort is internalized so deeply, they don't think for a second

I CAN'T EVEN COUNT THE AMOUNT OF TIMES I HEARD AND BELIEVED "GIRLS DON'T LIKE SEX" AS I WAS GROWING UP.

that the reason they feel this way could be because they're simply not attracted to men. After all, "girls just don't like sex".

It is socially acceptable for boys to watch porn and masturbate, so much so that they can discuss this without shame in social circles and conversations. Can you imagine talking about the "fantastic wank" you had in front of your friends as a teen, without feeling the guilt of societal slut-shaming heavy in your chest as you say it?

When we exist in a culture where women are ashamed to talk about their own pleasure this only further perpetuates the harmful narrative that we don't enjoy sex, because we are too ashamed to talk about it. The first time I spoke about masturbation with my friends felt akin to coming out, it was genuinely liberating and gave me a deep sense of validation, completely abandoning the internal shame I had been harbouring for years. It's not always easy to talk about taboo subjects but once we openly discuss them, the stigma-sting is taken out of them and they become a place of free discussion and exploration.

Not to be dramatic, but my first vibrator changed my mother-fucking life.

I bought it a few months after I was sexually assaulted. I didn't want what happened to me to take away the relationship I had spent years rebuilding with my body – I wanted to regain control. I wanted to reclaim my damn pussy and I wanted to love her again. I was fed up with feeling like she belonged to everyone but *herself.* I've had up to ten orgasms in one go with my vibrator, and buying this sex toy enabled me to claim back my body for myself. The body I had been shamed into hiding and reserving for men, and their gaze, my entire life. I once told an ex-boyfriend about the amazing orgasm I gave myself with a shower head using *that* setting, and he gave me the silent treatment for an hour. He eventually told me it was because it made him feel useless. Do you see how backwards it is? That it's "normal" for me to perform sexual acts for his gaze and in his company, but the moment I take control over *my own body* without a man in the room I am forced into some kind of "self-reflection treatment" and made to feel shame?

It is imperative that we normalize masturbation for *all* women. Because if we can normalize masturbation we also normalize female sexuality and with that, be viewed as people who enjoy sex too as opposed to passive objects to have sex *with*.

STOP JUDGING PEOPLE ON THEIR SEX LIVES

When it comes to having casual sex, a lot of us have been taught to think that "we don't wanna seem like *that* kind of girl, maybe we should hold out a little longer". Which is all part of the internalized misogynist trying to stop us living our best lives, while simultaneously slut-shaming other women who *are* that girl. There's nothing wrong with that girl, we love her! She is inside all of us. We want to see *more* women feel as though they are able to command their own lives and choose what's right for them, without feeling an ounce of guilt or shame.

A woman should have the right to choose what she wants for herself, just as men have the right to.

As a queer woman, dating people of different genders made me realize that casual sex can be a shame-free, beautiful, communicative and reciprocal experience as opposed to a *performance,* because it is free of gender roles. There's no cis het male gaze present during queer sex (at least, not a *physical* male gaze present). You step out of "performance" mode, and enter "do whatever

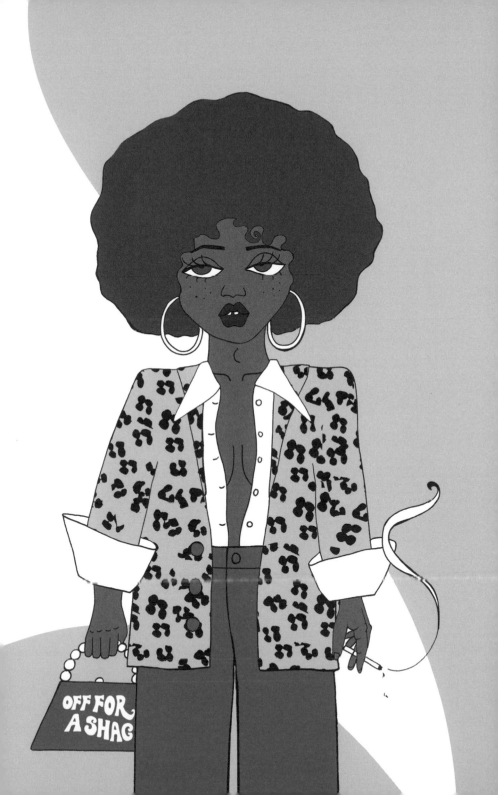

the fuck feels good" mode. It's also taught me that encounters without shame do exist. Know that you should never have to settle for anything less than *reciprocal, enthusiastic* and *consensual* sex. Yes, "even if it's casual"! This is the bare minimum. Not only that, *it is the law.*

If you have a vulva, buy yourself a hand mirror and promise me you will get to know it. It's frightening how many people have never seen their own genitals, or have no idea what they look like. A lot of the shame we have around pleasuring ourselves, or even prioritizing our orgasms during intercourse is because we don't even know what it looks like, let alone how to work it. So we don't bother communicating with our partner since we've been shamed into not acknowledging our need for pleasure. One of the most empowering things you can do for yourself is to reconnect with your body and learn about its anatomy. If there's one thing I wish I had had hammered into my skull as a young girl, it's that your body is *yours* and it belongs to *you* first, before it belongs to anyone else or their sexual desires.

If you have a clitoris, get to know it.

Neglecting the one part of your body that is designed exclusively to give you pleasure is an intentional effect of years living under patriarchy.

Rub your clit as a private act of resistance.

IF YOU HAVE A
CLITORIS
GET TO KNOW IT.

CHAPTER 12

IF IT'S NOT A "FUCK YES", IT'S A "NO"

A lot of people are reluctant to ask for consent because they feel like asking "kills the mood". But you know what *really* kills the mood? Sexually assaulting someone.

Taking a second to consider your partner and check that you're both on the same page shows maturity, high levels of emotional intelligence and respect for their boundaries. A person who's considerate of their partner's pleasure and consistently checks in to make sure they're comfortable exhibits high self-awareness. And that means that they're more likely to be aware of their *own* needs and desires. Self-awareness is, personally, such a turn on. What's hotter than a person who knows what they want and can confidently communicate these desires to their partner? Asking for consent is not only the law, it's very sexy.

Here are a few ways to ask for consent:
- "Do you like that?"
- "Can I take these off?"
- "Is this okay?"
- "Do you mind if we switch positions?"
- "Can I go down on you?"
- "How do you like it?"
- "Are you sure you feel ready for this, or would you prefer if we carried on kissing?"
- "Please know that you can say 'no' at any time."

Consent is mandatory, it is the law and it's not some form of flirting or foreplay. However, it can seamlessly fit into intercourse. Why not ask to remove their underwear while you're already kissing their neck, or whisper it in their ear? Or ask if they'd like to fuck you between kissing? It doesn't have to be the awkward and robotic script that it's been made out to be (unless that's your thing – we don't kink-shame in this family).

"WE DON'T HAVE TO DO ANYTHING TONIGHT"

As a survivor of sexual assault, nothing makes me feel more comfortable than when the person I'm intimate with creates an environment where I feel like at any point, I could say "no". When people ask and check in this takes the onus off you to have to *tell anyone* to stop. It relieves you of the pressure to feel like you have to do things you don't want to do.

For a lot of women who are used to a lifetime of being objectified, nothing feels sexier than safety.

RAPE CULTURE IS MAINTAINED BECAUSE WE FEAR THE CONSEQUENCES OF SIMPLY SAYING "NO" IN THE FIRST PLACE.

This means being able to do whatever you want in the bedroom, knowing that if you wanted it to stop *they would stop*. We don't empower women to feel that they're able to reject sexual advances. Rape culture is maintained because we fear the consequences of simply saying "no" in the first place.

We don't empower women to set boundaries and most of the time – unless they are *consciously* and *intentionally* implemented – they're nonexistent. The worst part is that for most women, it usually takes the most traumatic experiences to force them to learn what "boundaries" and "red flags" are in the first place, when they learn about them in therapy or through a conscious decision to heal *after* sexual trauma. One of the main reasons I'm writing this book is to introduce these concepts to people, hopefully before they have to learn the hard way like I did.

Many times people consent to sexual activity, because they fear what might happen if they reject the advances. But part of dismantling rape culture starts with encouraging women to set and *hold* boundaries, no matter the reaction they might receive. This is not victim blaming as the responsibility not to rape lies solely with the rapist. But if women aren't feeling empowered enough to say "no" in the first place, we will continue to foster a culture of coercion and "blurred lines". Consent is the only way to have sex. If there's no direct exchange of consent, it's rape:

- If you ask for consent and they hesitate or take a little longer to answer, reassure them by saying something like, "It's okay if you don't, would you prefer we just did x instead?"
- If they don't answer with a clear and enthusiastic "yes", it's a "no".
- "I'm tired" doesn't mean "convince me".
- "No" doesn't mean "keep asking *until I say 'yes'*."
- "No" is the most definable boundary in the world. There are no "blurred lines" when it comes to consent.

If it's not a "fuck yes", it's a "no".

THE RULES OF SEX

- Ask before doing something or progressing.
- Make sure if you want to have intercourse that your partner wants to have it with you too.
- If someone is asleep, unconscious, drunk or high they cannot consent to sex.
- Check in with someone every time you start a new sexual activity, whether that's going from oral sex to penetrative sex, or even switching up positions.
- Consenting to sex in the past or being in a relationship with someone does not automatically mean consent for the future. E.g. if Sam says he wants to have sex with Sally, but when it gets to it after 30 mins of foreplay Sam says he's too tired, Sally is not then entitled to have sex with Sam because he previously agreed. Sam can change his mind. He does not owe Sally sex.

SEX AND ALCOHOL

Sex is an experience, not a performance.

When it comes to sex we often feel this need to perform, and we all have our share of body insecurities and self-esteem issues. Whether it's your first time with a new partner or you don't really know what you're doing, it can feel a bit awkward and you might want a drink to take the edge off your anxiety and kick in a bit of confidence. But if you're drinking, remember that *drunk consent is not consent,* so sex with drunk consent is technically rape. If you're feeling anxious about wanting to sleep with someone or have low self-esteem when it comes to your body, you might want to try communicating this with your partner. It might seem scary to open up and be vulnerable, but there is nothing worse than waking up feeling confused and not being able to remember what happened "the night before".

SET SEX BOUNDARIES

We all have different boundaries, but it's important to check in and make sure that you're not slipping into disruptive habits. Here are a few red flags to memorize for the bedroom.

They refuse to wear a condom.

Dump them *on site*. If someone doesn't respect your body and the consequences you might face for the sake of their quick, short burst of pleasure –they've GOT to go. I mean it. If someone removes a condom during sex without your consent, this is sexual assault. There are plenty of people out there who are willing to respect your boundaries – people ignoring your desires and safety is not normal, it's just been *normalized*.

They're only nice to you during sex, or after you've had sex.

They're using you – you're not a person to them, you're an object. Also, if they're only hitting you up late hours, it means you're their quick-fix and they only want you when they're bored. Casual sex is totally fine, and you should be able to enjoy it without shame just like men. But if you feel like deep down you're accepting casual sex from someone when you want a relationship with them (settling for crumbs when you want the cake, see page 47), then stop settling for it. Reserve that energy for someone who can meet *all* of your needs, because it's what you deserve.

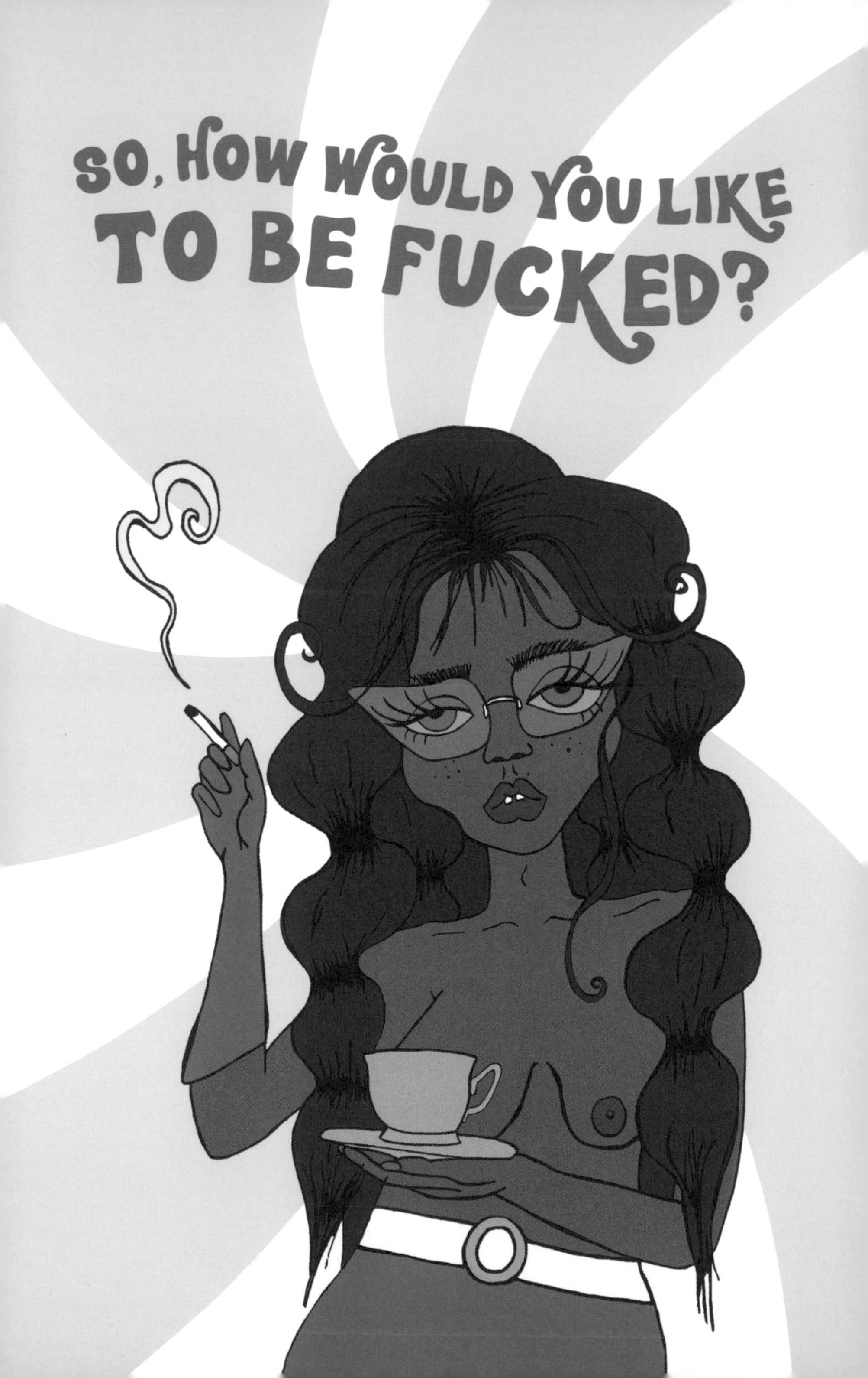
SO, HOW WOULD YOU LIKE
TO BE FUCKED?

They call you demeaning names.
Unless previously agreed that these names are okay for you, if someone starts calling you "slut", "whore" or "bitch" during intercourse, this is a big red flag. Especially if you've asked them to stop and they continue, it shows an enormous lack of respect towards you and your body. Do they even see a person at all, if this is what they're calling you? Most of this behaviour is re-enactment of porn and it's not a sign of an emotionally healthy partner.

They perform *any* sexual act on you without asking first.
Sure, sex can flow naturally and we can pay attention to the person's body language to see where things might be going. But consenting to a kiss doesn't mean you're consenting to oral sex. Just because you're having a nice big sloppy snog on the sofa, it doesn't mean it automatically "leads to fingering" because "That wAs the VibE". Ask first.

They use guilt and shame.
If someone makes you feel guilty for not having sex, or for not liking the same things as they do, or uses your insecurities to make you do things – *goodbye.*

They expect you to pay for emergency contraception.
Despite both people being equally responsible for unsafe and unprotected sex, people with vaginas are always expected to pay the price for birth control, emergency contraception and morning after pills because it's seen as "our problem". This person doesn't care about you enough if they can't share the responsibility.

OTHER FORMS OF CONSENT

The truth is that respecting people's boundaries goes beyond sex. An ex-boyfriend once drew on my body and took pictures of me while I was sleeping. Men physically put their hands on my waist to "gesture" that I need to move out of the way, instead of politely asking me to move. Women treat me like an agony aunt and come up to me in the toilets, offloading their trauma, expecting me to offer therapy in the cubicle.

Our relationship with boundaries, whether setting our own or respecting other people's, depends on our upbringing and re-enacting our earliest relationships from childhood out of our subconscious. While this *explains* our lack of boundaries, it does not *excuse* them. We must actively work to rewrite what we know to develop healthier boundaries, so we're able to maintain better relationships with others and ourselves.

Here are some ways people violate boundaries:
- Asking someone to do something more than once, after they've already said "no". By doing this, you push the person into feeling pressured to compromise their boundaries to please *you* and betray *themselves*.
- Entering someone's bedroom without permission (depending on the relationship).
- Taking pictures of people without consent (when someone is sleeping, walking on the street and so on).
- Borrowing people's things without asking first.
- Reading people's phones without their consent.
- Touching people's hair without consent.
- Offloading your problems onto friends, strangers or people on the internet without checking in first.
- Helping someone without checking first to see if they want help.
- Giving unsolicited advice to someone who never asked for it.

- Pursuing someone who has given adequate signals that they're not interested or that the relationship has ended.
- Outing you to someone as LGBTQ+.

Having a lack of boundaries doesn't just mean you're more susceptible to accept things that aren't good for you, it also means you're likely to exhibit toxic behaviours yourself that could cause harm to someone else.

Here are some signs that you have unhealthy boundaries:
- You touch other people without asking.
- You go against your own personal beliefs and values to please other people. E.g. taking drugs on a night out because everyone else is doing it, even though you don't usually do them.
- You fall in love with someone new very quickly. It's a sign that you're seeking validation and need something to make you feel whole. You can't love someone you know nothing about.
- You offload your life story and your traumas to someone when you first meet them.
- You find it hard to say "no".
- You give as much as you can for the sake of giving without asking for reciprocity, because you struggle to communicate your desires.
- You subconsciously seek partners who need fixing and healing.
- You constantly excuse someone's mistreatment of you – "they're only like this when they're drunk."
- You protect people who are doing damage to you.

I had to end a toxic relationship when I realized the treatment I had allowed and accepted from someone meant that my boundaries had become non-existent. I had allowed my boundaries to be worn down over years to accept a love that was less than I deserved.

The ultimate act of self-love is to know when to walk away from a toxic relationship and, although hard, this is you actively practising self-care, self-preservation and self-worth. It's a powerful agent in your steps towards self-empowerment. It's you choosing yourself and acknowledging that there is a way out of repetitively involving yourself with the same toxic people.

It's never too late to set boundaries with people in your life, and if they don't respect them?

I hope you love yourself enough to walk away.

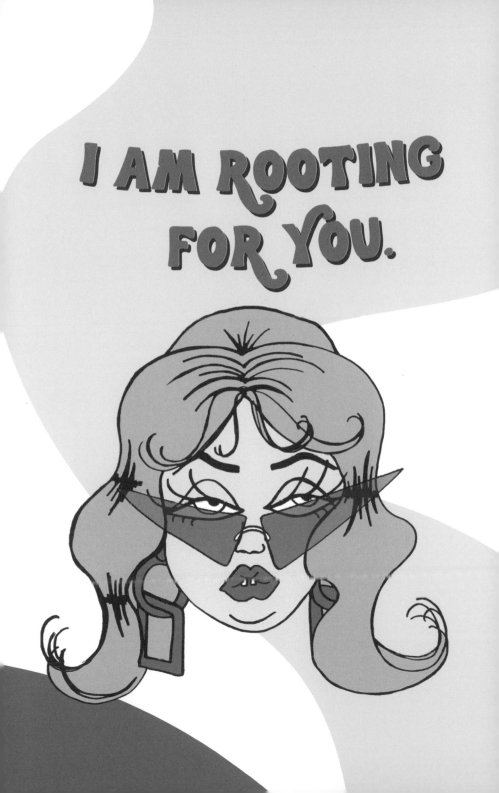

CHAPTER 13

"WHAT DID SHE EXPECT, GOING OUT LIKE THAT?"

TRIGGER WARNING: MENTION OF INSTANCES OF SEXUAL ASSAULT AND RAPE

It shouldn't be normalized to experience discomfort, fear or aggression during intercourse. It shouldn't be normalized to just "roll over" and "give in" when we have already said "no", or said nothing at all.

Maybe one day I'll "tell my story", but I don't think details are important. For now, I'll just say "me too" and use this space in my book to pass on the lessons I had to learn the hard way. However, I'm afraid there's one thing I *can't* teach you – I can't teach you how to avoid sexual assault. It's not something anyone can avoid by taking protective measures, because sexual assault is *never* your fault.

Having "uncomfortable sex" is often accepted as a necessary introduction to womanhood. This sense of "girls not enjoying sex" makes uncomfortable experiences feel *normal*. That is why the term "rape culture" is used – it describes the social culture fostered that normalizes and justifies rape:

- Rape culture is reinforced by idioms such as "boys will be boys" to excuse men's actions, and insinuating that there are "blurred lines" when it comes to consent with lyrics such as "I know you want it".
- Rape jokes are used as a form of male bonding.
- The fact America elected a president who bragged about sexual assault and "grabbing women by the pussy", and spoke out about the fact that he could do this because of his position of power.
- The preventative measures we are encouraged to take to "avoid" being raped, instead of taking measures to stop people from raping in the first place. These include "covering up", buying rape whistles, never walking home alone, moving to an apartment where you can see who's at the door before they can see you, carrying keys between your fingers, not making eye contact with men, packing an extra layer for the walk home, lying about where you live, choosing shoes in case you need to run, avoiding jewellery that makes a noise and draws attention, deciding who you give your number to, making sure there's something in your purse to fight off an attacker.
- Rapists rarely ever see a prison cell. In 2018, only 1.7 per cent of rape allegations in the UK resulted in a charge.

ONE OF THE "NICE GUYS", HUH?

Rape culture spins the narrative that "nice guys" don't rape. But they do. In fact, 90 per cent of all rape perpetrators are already known to the victim[*].

These "monsters" we imagine and spend our entire lives being taught to avoid in the streets and in dark alleyways, *are actually already in our lives.* They have sisters, mothers, friends, careers, families – you might even share a bed with them. This harmful

[*] Glasgow University study, reported on BBC Online, "Sex attack victims usually know attacker, says new study", 1 March 2018. https://www.bbc.co.uk/news/uk-scotland-43128350

narrative – that we need to "look out" for rapists on the streets, when they're usually already in our lives – is an enormous component of rape culture, and puts the onus back on the victim to take every precaution to "prevent" rape happening to them.

Our society has an innate urge to use women as scapegoats, in an attempt to justify rapists' actions and avoid holding them accountable. One of the most harmful types of misogyny is the belief that victims who speak up about their experience of sexual assault have in one way or another "asked for it". But let's be clear here, it is physically impossible to "ask" for rape.

The way people interrogate rape victims is almost like a checklist:
- "Did you definitely say 'no'?"
- "Did you push them off?"
- "Did you not lead them on?"

If you didn't take all the preventative measures, they believe it's your fault.

There's a world of silence that's quietly and insidiously enabling a system of sexual violence to continue. However, cracks are beginning to show. Through #MeToo, the movement founded by Tarana Burke, more victims are speaking up. Slowly our secret, disgusting reality is being revealed. An *apocalypse* would occur if every single person guilty of rape and sexual assault was outed – society would not know how to cope with the realization that so many people they know and love are complicit and have committed rape. In fact rape is so normalized, people don't even realize they themselves have committed it.

In order for it to stop, there need to be open conversations *now* about what has happened, how we can stop it from happening again, and making it clear from a young age what does and doesn't constitute consent. Because when sexual violence isn't openly discussed, it becomes normalized. And when it becomes normalized, it becomes accepted. And when something becomes accepted, it leads to the culture we are currently living in where

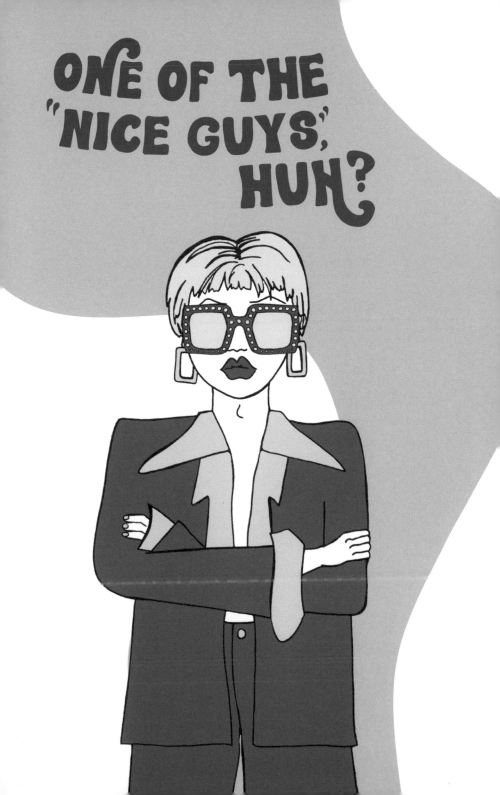

people are being raped and committing rape – without even knowing that it's rape. When something is normalized it forces the victim to question if what happened to them is a big enough deal to speak out against. But it is a big deal. Sexual assault is always a big deal.

There was no one I felt I could talk to about my experiences of sexual assault, until I founded my online community and quickly realized I wasn't the only one. We live in a society that functions on our silence and we are immersed in a culture that perpetuates it. If we dare to speak out, we unravel years of carefully woven structures that are in place to protect men and their actions, which they are still yet to be held accountable for. This is why victims don't speak out. *Everything* is stacked against them, encouraging them to keep their mouths shut.

SOME THINGS AREN'T NORMAL, THEY HAVE BEEN *NORMALIZED.* THERE'S A DIFFERENCE.

When we have said that we're "too tired", when we have asked them to "stop", when we haven't given communicative consent. It's easy to blame rape culture on the fact that consent is only recently being discussed in *some* schools, but what kind of a person still wants to have sex with someone who has verbally expressed disinterest, *whether they were taught consent or not*? Someone who looks uncomfortable, someone who is scared. Yes, consent is not taught in many schools, but the problem is also deeply entrenched because of the extreme and violent types of porn that are widely available to (not to mention produced by and for) men. We live in a culture that breeds and encourages toxic masculinity, at the expense of women and our bodies. But I'm bored of blaming the "culture" that rapists were raised in. We forget that *people* are culture – and it's time to hold these people accountable for their actions.

STOP INTERROGATING RAPE VICTIMS

If someone talks to you about their experience of rape or sexual assault, never ask them why they didn't report it. Never ask them why they're not fighting it. Treat people as experts on their own experiences and believe them. Blaming the victim is a system that men created to avoid accountability, and it's a system that they can perpetuate happily with legal backing. In the US, only 2 per cent of reported rapists ever see a prison cell (and if you include unreported accounts it's actually 0.5 per cent of rapists that go to jail)*.

It's the only crime where we interrogate the victim as though they were the perpetrator. You wouldn't ask someone who was robbed, "Why didn't you fight the attacker off?" because as a society we understand and respect that other people's personal possessions are not for others to take without consent. *Duh!* But when it comes to sexual assault, we still believe that women's bodies exist solely for male consumption. If she's walking home late at night? *It's up for grabs.* It's almost seen as a right that because she was out there "in the wild", that a man can come along and use her body for his pleasure. Because "that's what women's bodies are for". Think about that for a second. We respect other people's wallets and materialistic possessions, and treat reports of theft to the police more seriously than we do the rape of women's *bodies.* Bodies which are now traumatised, violated and carrying the heavy burden of silence for the rest of their lives.

Things to avoid saying to a victim of sexual assault:
- "Did you definitely say 'no'?"
- "What were you wearing?"
- "Did you try to fight them off?"
- "Why haven't you reported it? They can't get away with this."
- "Be careful about reporting it, you could ruin their career."

* "The Criminal Justice System: Statistics", Rape, Abuse & Incest National Network website, https://www.rainn.org/statistics/criminal-justice-system

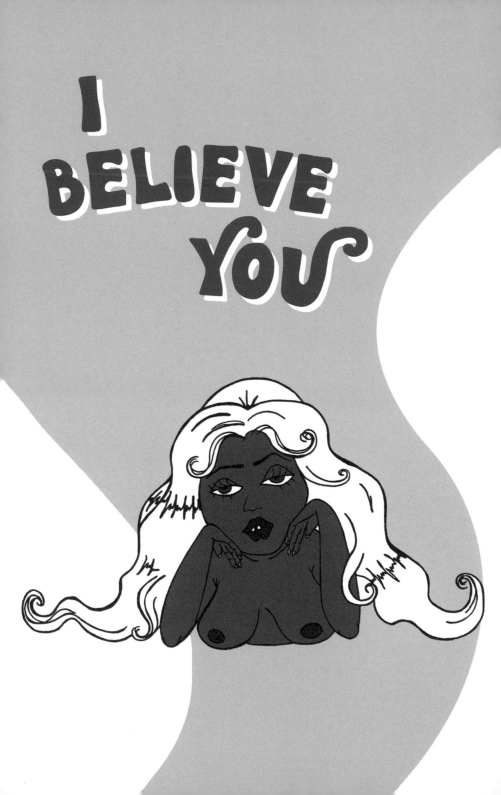

- "Are you *sure* it was rape?"
- "Did they definitely hear you say 'no'?"
- "If there was no struggle, how is it rape?"
- "Somebody really wanted to have sex with *you*?"

Affirming things to say to a victim of sexual assault:
- "Thank you for trusting me with your story."
- "I believe you."
- "How can I support you?"
- "However you handle this situation, I support your decision."
- "You didn't deserve this."

People are so quick to ask survivors why we didn't report it, without realizing there are systems and people *every step of the way* to ensure this never happens – *even* when we do try to reach out. The system fails so many rape victims every single day. Rape is the most under-reported crime and, after my experience, I finally understood why. I told a person of authority the day after it happened, and they encouraged me not to report it because they said "I'd think twice, this might ruin his career". Months later, I decided I would ignore this advice and I got the courage up to report it anyway. I went to a sexual assault clinic to talk to the police and they told me there was "nothing they could do", and that there would be "no point" in reporting it.

So, I'm writing to you to be the person I needed in that moment. To remind you that if you're worried the truth might "destroy a man's career" – fuck his career. That's on him, *he* should have thought about that before he to tried to take what didn't belong to him.

Go ahead. I believe you.

TRIGGER
WARNING:
MENTION OF
INSTANCES OF
SEXUAL ASSAULT

CHAPTER 14

WOMEN DO NOT EXIST TO SATISFY THE MALE GAZE

"A man in a room full of women is ecstatic. A woman in a
room full of men is terrified." – Unknown

It costs *more* to be a woman, in the same world where we are paid
substantially *less* than men, and we're tricked into believing that "splitting
the bill" is the route to equality? Regardless of your gender, this should
make your blood *boil*. This eye-opening perspective on patriarchy was first
introduced to me by author and activist Chidera Eggerue, and I haven't
stopped thinking about it since.

Here are just a few examples of the tax we end up paying for misogyny,
and how the presence of the heterosexual male gaze limits our experience
in this society:

- We choose our route home based not on efficiency, but on which route
  is less likely to have men lurking around who will potentially harass or
  assault us.
- We give a fake name and number to a guy who won't leave us alone in

a bar, or say that we have a boyfriend, because we fear what he might do if we just say "no".

- The money we spend on preventative measures "just in case" – rape alarms, pepper spray, tazers.

- The money we spend on contraceptive measures and morning-after pills. The responsibility of keeping sex safe and correcting mistakes is almost always down to us.

- Queer women are not able to show displays of affection in public because of the sexualized response from men, and the unwanted attention it attracts. Girl-on-girl love in public is always assumed to be a "performance" for men.

- Constant vigilance and awareness of our every move in public, to avoid giving men "the wrong idea". Everything is calculated, we rarely get to just *be*.

- The resources of time, energy and money that go into being "presentable" (aka "desirable" by racist, fatphobic, transphobic beauty standards) so that we are met with basic human respect – shaving our bodies (our razors are also more expensive than men's), applying our make-up and doing our hair in the mornings. Of course, this is all a choice. No one is *forcing a razor to our armpits*. But if we don't pay in *prettiness*, we just end up paying the price of unsolicited comments about our appearance. We cannot win either way. This is made particularly hard for marginalized women who occupy bodies that are deemed less "desirable".

- The money we spend on cars and taxis to get home safely, when men and people with male-passing privilege have the option to just walk home or take the bus, because they don't fear being attacked or raped.

- If we do decide to walk home, we often pack an extra layer or an entire different outfit to wear to and from the club/bar.
- Any applied effort to our appearance as women is considered an "invitation" for men to start talking to us, so we often dress ourselves down or cover ourselves up to avoid receiving unsolicited remarks. Even then, if this isn't effective we police our body language.
- The male gaze has sexualized and objectified our bodies so much that they have been shamed of their inherent use, to function. People who have periods hide sanitary products and feel ashamed of our periods when we need to go to the bathroom.
- Getting off public transport early because we have been harassed/ made to feel uncomfortable, as the threat of someone following us home if we get off at our *actual* destination is very real.
- The embarrassment/shame of breastfeeding in public.

The consequences of the male gaze are exhausting and expensive. We spend money and energy keeping ourselves safe from men, and yet still – we are paid less than them.

"The male gaze" is a term coined by Laura Mulvey to describe the way women are portrayed as objects in the media. It has insidiously permeated every facet of our lives and identities. From the films we watch, all the way down to our craving for its validation.

Everyday rituals –applying make-up, shaving, doing our hair and choosing our clothes – are all decisions subconsciously filtered through the desires of the all-powerful male gaze.

These are the rituals that we are expected to perform in order to be treated with the same respect men are afforded for showing up just as they are.

EVERYDAY
BEAUTY RITUALS
ARE SUBCONSCIOUSLY
FILTERED
THROUGH THE
THE DESIRES
OF THE
ALL-POWERFUL
MALE GAZE

It all comes down to our bodies and our desirability, no matter what we do, who we are or what we achieve. The expectation to perform prettiness is laid on even thicker again, for marginalized women (see page 32).

BODY POLITICS

I have a very confusing relationship with my body; there are times when I feel as though it doesn't belong to me. Equally, there are times when I genuinely do not feel safe in my *own body*. How awful is that? The one place you're supposed to call home feels like an unsafe place to inhabit. Maybe it's because the perceptions I have about it are based on hetero male gaze standards and not my own, or because I have been sexually assaulted, or because my body is groped and chucked around at night clubs, or because cisgender men dominate conversations about what we are afforded in reproductive rights. Or it could be because the shape of my stomach has been discussed between hundreds of men in comment sections on YouTube. There really are a multitude of experiences and events I can pinpoint in my life where I have been told, with words or with non-consensual actions, that my body doesn't belong to me. The world thinks it's up for grabs, depending on my choice of clothing, and up for discussion just by *existing*.

What kind of a relationship are we expected to have with our own bodies, if not a conflictual one, when we are socialized to believe that they exist for male consumption? We are taught that men are entitled to our bodies so much so that we are blamed for being assaulted because of our choice of clothing, but *still* expected to present in a way which is desirable enough for them to look at, in order to receive respect and acknowledgement. The mixed messages we receive about our bodies make us incredibly vulnerable to capitalism, as we are encouraged to buy solutions to fix our biological "flaws". It becomes easier to navigate our distorted perceptions of our bodies once we understand that a lot of the normalized beauty rituals are a direct result of capitalism, and not actual human "flaws". Flaws don't exist. Capitalism exists. But because capitalism exists within most human interactions in society, these flaws have been legitimized. The insecurity of body hair on women, for example, was a seed planted by male advertisers in 1915, because they realized they could make money selling razors to women. Before then women didn't shave, it simply wasn't something we felt insecure about. But they planted the seed of insecurity and then filled a gap in the market. Voila! We've been trained and socialized to be disgusted by our own bodies for male consumption and capitalist profit.

THE MALE GAZE ACTIVELY LIMITS AND RESTRICTS YOUR EXPERIENCE ON THIS PLANET

The limitations that the male gaze have imposed on my life is one of the main reasons that I go to therapy. It manifests as an anxiety in my stomach and makes me short of breath when I walk down the street at night, and at times during the day too. Additionally, there's the anxiety for my safety that comes when I'm on a date with another woman. When you're on a queer date there's no "seizing the moment" that you get on hetero dates. When it comes to kissing or any form of affection, you scan the room for lurking eyes, and have to check that it's a safe place for you and the person you're with. I also tend to check in with the person I'm on a date with to see if it's okay, because for obvious reasons, some people aren't as comfortable being visibly queer. There have been times when I wanted to kiss someone in public, and if wasn't specifically at a queer safe space or there were people around, we've had to kill the moment and go somewhere else, just to kiss.

Being visibly queer in the UK isn't as safe as the media will have you believe, and when you're two queer girls on a date, you can bet that at least once you'll be approached by men who think you're just friends. In my experience, it's even worse when I'm a date with another femme. *After all, what could two girls possibly be doing looking like that at a bar, if not for male attention?* I have literally been holding the hand of a girl at a bar and had a man come over trying to chat her up, and when I told him we were on a date he went, "Don't worry, that's hot! I'm into that!"

I swear to God – you cut men and they *bleed* audacity.

HOW MUCH OF MY FEMININITY IS WHO I TRULY AM, AND HOW MUCH OF IT IS A PRODUCT OF PATRIARCHAL BRAINWASHING TO EXIST FOR MALE CONSUMPTION?

When I think about who *Florence Given* really is, I imagine that she's locked deep inside of me, hidden, waiting to be revealed. She's feeling suffocated, wrapped inside the false narratives that have told her who she should be since birth.

I can't help but wonder how much of my identity is just a product of layers and layers of coping mechanisms developed to survive years of emotional abuse, toxic relationships and existing under patriarchy. How are we ever supposed to know who we really are if our entire existence has already been decided for us the moment we were assigned male or female genders at birth? If we have been brainwashed to identify with our assigned binary gender? How are we supposed to know how much of our identity is constructed or real, and how much of it is a product of the society we were brought up in? Where we have been force-fed heteronormative narratives, and taught to present ourselves in a way that is both desirable and acceptable?

The ways our decisions are controlled by the male gaze are so insidious, we don't even realize that it affects the choices we make on a daily basis.

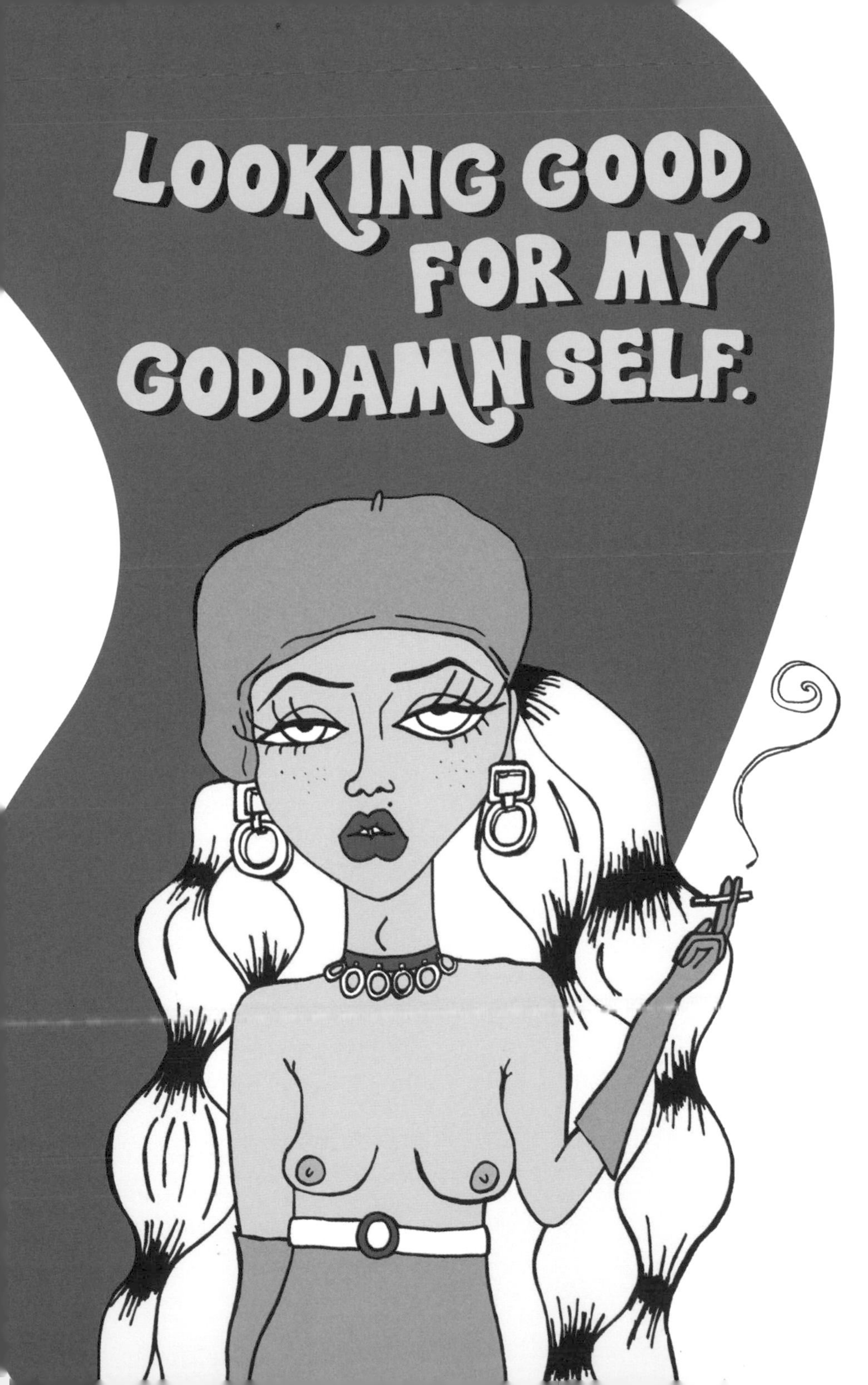
LOOKING GOOD
FOR MY
GODDAMN SELF.

In the eyes of society, the more feminine we are the more "desirable" we are, and having desirability as a woman gives us the privilege of being acknowledged and visible.

Not to mention that "femininity" as a standard anyway is measured by a woman's proximity to whiteness and Eurocentric features. Our collective idea of "pretty" in the first place is inherently racist. We know that in theory we could turn up to work without make-up – no one's *forcing* us to wear make-up to work. But we know that we are treated better if we do. The cultural narrative is so strong that even as women we internalize it, and it says that if women are not desirable nor able to satisfy men, we are worthless. This is why most of us have such low self-esteem and fucking *hate* ourselves – because we are not living out our most authentic lives.

There are so many ways that we bear the consequences of patriarchy, and what's frustrating is that we are expected to show up in a way that pleases men just to exist in this world and to be treated with the respect we deserve. This costs money. Capitalism turns us all into objects of desire yet also expects us to pay the price to fit into this accepted vision, without questioning if that version of us aligns with our *own* desires. Never are we asked about how we want to look for our own visual satisfaction. But as long as we don't question the status quo and continue not to challenge the ways patriarchy affects our lives, we prolong our collective suffering.

If you ever uncover parts of yourself that make you feel electric, in a world that thrives and evolves at the expense of your insecurities, please cherish them. These are *your* best bits. These are your best bits untouched by social conditioning. This is *your* identity. Be proud, for they are the parts of yourself that blossomed and survived despite years of assimilation. These parts make you iconic.

CENSORED

One of the most confusing messages we receive about our bodies is that we are told our worth is tied to our ability to be sexy and desirable, that our bodies are available to be used to sell products, that we are valuable when we pose naked, thin and airbrushed next to a perfume bottle to generate profit for large companies – but once we are seen to be harnessing that power for *ourselves*, once we are seen taking control of our own sexuality, we are a threat. A woman who has no shame of her sexuality, who knows her own power and is capable of harnessing her objectification for her own financial gain or self-empowerment is a threat to capitalism and the status quo. She's also an absolute fucking icon.

Enter, the all-powerful and insidious tool of violence – shame.

Shame does not want you to have autonomy over your own body, because society relies on having control over your body as its product – and products aren't supposed to feel "empowered", *they're products*. Shame is the tool that stops you from exploring self-pleasure and masturbation, because it means you might realize you don't need men for sex. Shame exists in the form of calling women "bitchy" to make us feel embarrassed for speaking up and setting boundaries, keeping us vulnerable and easier to manipulate. Shame exists in the form of censoring women's nipples. Shame is weaponized to make sure we are never aware of our power. The world does not want you to wake up to the fact it is profiting from your subjugation, shame and insecurities. It doesn't want you to tap into your inherent power.

Not only are our bodies used as sites of objectification and breeding grounds for insecurities, but they are heavily sexualized, often before we've even hit puberty. I was branded "sexual" before I'd even had sex. Before I'd even done so much as kissed someone, I was told that my skirt length was distracting to male teachers, but that I couldn't wear trousers because they were for the boys. Equally, boys were unfairly not allowed to wear skirts. In other words, the message I was told and deeply internalized was: be desirable, be feminine, but not so much that men think of you in that way. Oh, and if you want to wear trousers, sorry sweetie but ThoSe arE FoR BoYs!

So much shame is embedded in our bodies. Told to put ourselves on display for the gaze and financial profit of others, but *never* our own. In some places showing nipples is still illegal. Not all nipples of course! Just female nipples. But nipples aren't sexual. They're sexualized. A sexual gaze has been unwillingly thrust onto female nipples.

Inner observation task: Think about something you've always wanted to experiment with in your appearance, and ask yourself why you've never done it.

What parts of your self-expression feel like a routine?

What parts of the way you express yourself feel *electric*?

In what ways have you internalized the male gaze in your standards of beauty, and sexualized women's bodies?

For example, I'd spent the majority of my adolescence wearing body-tight clothing because I'd internalized the message that women are to be trophy-esque figures of desirability. My friends and I wore uncomfortable bodycon dresses we couldn't sit down in, paired with painfully high heels to parties. We taped our tits up to make them look bigger, wore shapewear under our dresses so we didn't have to spend the whole evening holding in our stomachs, and we had cuts on our legs from shaving close enough to remove every last prickle.

I was wearing shapewear, shaving my legs, stuffing my bra and battling an eating disorder at 14 years old. I was taught that for women to be seen as desirable, we must experience discomfort. The phrase "Beauty is Pain" stuck with me – and it hurt me.

As soon as I came out as bisexual to my friends and family, I felt room to breathe. To question *everything*.

> **I asked myself for the first time who the hell
> I was even doing this painful performance for.
> Was I "doing it for me" or was I doing it be
> acknowledged by the male gaze?
> The answer: both.**

The influence of the male gaze was so strong I had mistaken it for my own idea of beauty. Shortly after I acknowledged this, I allowed myself to wear more baggy clothing – and I started to feel *electric* in my gender expression. I felt both sexy *and* comfortable, something I didn't even know was possible.

I feel electric when I wear a suit, but I feel equally euphoric wearing nothing but a pair of leopard-print platforms. The difference is that now I view my gender expression as something that is constantly refining itself, finding ways to connect back to who I was before I was *told* to be someone else.

Think about what makes you feel alive in your body and jot down those moments as they rise in your life.

WHAT PARTS OF YOUR SELF-EXPRESSION FEEL LIKE A ROUTINE, AND WHAT PARTS MAKE YOU FEEL ELECTRIC?

Outer observation task: The next time you watch a film, pay attention to how the female characters are positioned. Is the focus on the woman all about her desirability and curves? Does she even have much to say, or have they given all the important lines to the male actors? Does her character reinforce sexist stereotypes about women? Does she "risk everything for love" and won't stop talking about relationships? Google "examples of male gaze" and you will find plenty of ways women feel objectified for the way they look, as opposed to their male counterparts who are acknowledged for their achievements.

If you want to see the double-standard of how men and women are expected to show up in the world, just watch the dynamics of an awards show. You'll see women with three people holding up their dresses just to get on stage, targeted ads on Instagram will try to sell you diet tea so you can attain her "event-ready figure", but the backstage footage will show that she was in fact wrapped by a team of people in cling film just to get her into her corset. All the while, male attendees slip effortlessly into their suit and tie.

After all, men are invited to these events to win a trophy – not become one.

CHAPTER 15

STOP PUTTING PEOPLE ON A PEDESTAL

"A pedestal is as much a prison as any small, confined space."
– Gloria Steinem

We cannot fall in love with the idea that we have created of someone, and then feel disappointed when they don't turn out to be the person we *assumed* they were. This disappointment isn't justified. You're not entitled to feel let down by someone for not matching the fictitious narrative you have written about them and projected from *your own mind*.

When we think of projection, we usually associate it with projecting our insecurities onto other people. However that isn't always the case. Another form of insecurity projection manifests in how we put certain people on a pedestal in our lives. We often idolize people who highlight something we feel we are lacking within ourselves.

Putting someone on a pedestal dehumanizes them, because we expect the impossible of this person and don't give them a chance to be a multifaceted flawed human. With the expectation of perfection, comes inevitable disappointment.

The person who has been placed on a pedestal feels pressure to perform and act in a certain way to avoid failure and letting you down. They fear you won't love them if you "knew the real them", or if they dared to be vulnerable and let down their guard in front of you. By placing someone on a pedestal you actually prevent yourself from forming a meaningful relationship with this person.

Now, there's a difference between putting someone on a pedestal and holding them in high regard.

When you put someone on a pedestal, you place yourself below them and project onto them the parts of yourself that you feel you lack. You might even betray your own beliefs and boundaries just to please them.

We secretly believe that "greatness" exists outside of ourselves, unwilling to acknowledge and nurture our own talents to avoid the uncomfortable truth that we don't actually know ourselves or what we want from life. Emulating our role models is one thing, but living a life by a certain narrative we believe they would approve of against our own beliefs is another. If we don't feel that we are capable of growing, becoming successful or honing our own skills, the next best thing is to cling to a person *who is*.

HOW TO TAKE SOMEONE OFF A PEDESTAL

If you can feel that you're putting someone above yourself, it's an indication that you need to do some digging and figure out what it is you feel you're lacking. If someone's presence makes you feel insecure or brings out an ugly jealousness in you, your inner child is asking to be looked after and nurtured. So tend to them.

- Practise the self-love rituals on page 217. You must build a stronger sense of self and your own identity. We imitate people who emulate the levels of beauty, self-awareness, creativity and confidence we aspire to achieve, but how are we ever supposed to know who we really are if we're constantly living in someone else's shadow, trying to act in ways that we believe they would approve of? No one's imaginary approval is ever worth compromising your own boundaries and beliefs for.

- Think about what makes you come alive and what ignites a fire inside of you – *and do more of that.* Follow that feeling. When you're used to defining your success against another person's, you can lose sight of what it is *you* actually want to achieve in life. *This is why you are stagnant!* What makes another person feel happy and fulfilled won't do the same for you. It's entirely impossible to copy someone's process and achieve the same results.

- Realize that the person you're pedestalling has their own person on a pedestal above them too. Wild, right? Because they're human, flawed, full of projections, insecurities and need therapy, just like you.

- Realize that people don't owe you *shit.* People don't owe you "nice" and people don't owe it to you to perform the part of themselves that you fell in love with. The world owes you nothing, and equally you owe it nothing. Remember these words to keep your ego in check every now and then.

Burn your idols, take them off the pedestal – and if *I'm* on your pedestal, in the words of Roxane Gay "*consider me already knocked off*".

You're not in love with them, they are just mirroring back to you the greatness that already exists within yourself. Tap into that power.

NO ONE'S APPROVAL IS EVER WORTH **COMPROMISING** YOUR OWN BOUNDARIES AND ABANDONING YOUR OWN BELIEFS FOR.

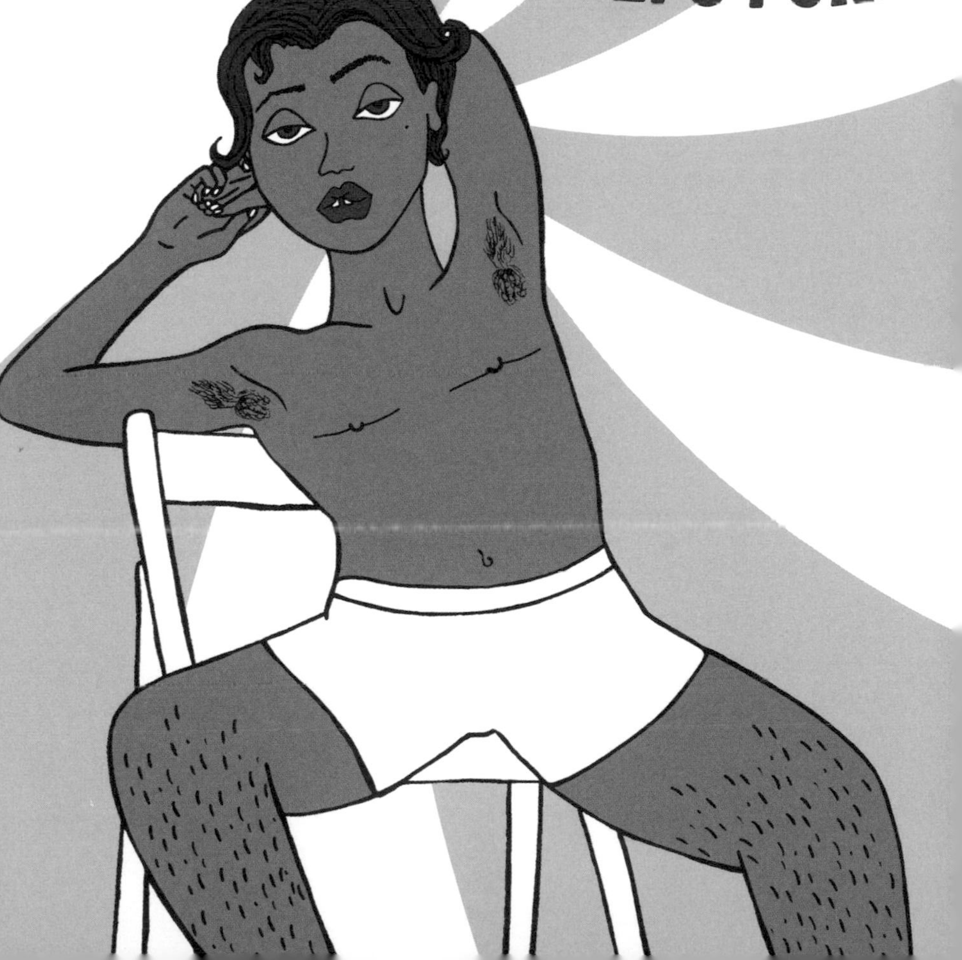

CHAPTER 16

LIFE'S SHORT, DUMP THEM

Dump them. Why? Because you always deserve *better*.

Every day, I receive hundreds of messages asking for relationship advice. But I never reply to a single one of them. The answer is, and always will be, the same.

Because life is too short to remain in an unfulfilling relationship for the sake of staying in your comfort zone. Your new life is waiting for you. Stop shrinking yourself, shed your skin and watch how you blossom and evolve. Watch how you become an even more refined version of the already incredible person you are, outside of a relationship where you're encouraged to view yourself as someone's "other half". Sometimes the dead bits we cut off to encourage growth are our split ends – and sometimes, it's a whole husband.

If you have to ask whether or not you should stay with someone who leaves your messages on read, leaves mess around the house for you to clean up or has a tendency to lie – you already know the answer, you just want someone to *tell you* that you deserve better. While breaking up with someone who has a history of toxic behaviour may seem like the obvious thing to do, so many people stay in these relationships because they don't believe there's going to be another love after them, and they just don't believe that they deserve better. They have learned to associate romantic love with *compromising*. I was that person. I didn't have anyone in my life telling me that I deserved better. I had no one telling me that while I was settling for crumbs, someone out there wanted to give me the whole damn cake. However, I also *intentionally* ignored and dismissed content on Instagram with #DumpHim messaging when I was in a relationship, *because I knew I would be faced with the truth that I was settling.* In the words of Chidera Eggerue, whose relentless campaigning against settling for shit men inspired me to be vocal about my own experiences – I was "actively ignoring this advice *to my own detriment*".

No one likes to be told they deserve better, because it means acknowledging that you have to change. But you are allowed to unapologetically break up with people, based on the simple fact that they are not enough. Give yourself that permission.

A lot of people stay in relationships out of fear of being single, and debilitatingly low self-worth. But here's the beautiful thing about being single – take a second to think about how incredibly unique you are already. Think about all of your interests, your music taste, the clothes you wear, how you do your make-up in the morning if at all, think of all the parts that make up the unique person you are. By choosing to focus on yourself and choosing to be intentionally single, you are only going to become a more *refined* version of yourself. A whole, refined, evolving bitch. By being single you are only going to become more of the person the world has kept you from becoming, by conditioning you to fit into its boring, binary system. The glow-up that ensues after a good dumping is so hideously fantastic, you won't even recognize yourself.

There's nothing to be afraid of – walk into your own arms.

STOP RAISING HIM, HE'S NOT YOUR SON

Do you find yourself pouring endless amounts of energy into your partner, in the hope that he will grow into the person you want him to be?

Does it ever feel like you've adopted a child in a man's body?

Does your relationship feel draining?

Do you book his appointments?

Do you make sure he gets to places on time?

Do you clean up after him?

Are you his mum?

No? So stop raising him.

While my message of not settling for less than you deserve does apply to any couple regardless of gender, I decided to intentionally fuel the existing #DumpHim movement, because there is a very specific type of settling that happens in heterosexual relationships. This desperately needed addressing, and I was unconsciously engaging in it for years myself. As women we are socialized to be "nurturers" and caregivers, and we often end up dating men that fill the role of the person *receiving* that care. We have been told our whole lives that relationships are about compromise, but what you should never have to compromise is *yourself*. Because compromising yourself isn't "compromise" at all – it's self-betrayal. There are people in the world who would kill to spend an evening in a restaurant in your presence, but you're too busy seeing the "potential" in your boyfriend, who refuses to get a job because he thinks his band (who haven't played a single gig yet) is going to single-handedly "change the music industry". There are people out there who are willing to respect your boundaries and engage in a reciprocal relationship, but you're too busy booking your boyfriend's doctor appointments, doing his laundry and covering his rent? Women are not rehabilitation centres for men who want to grow, evolve and reach their final form.

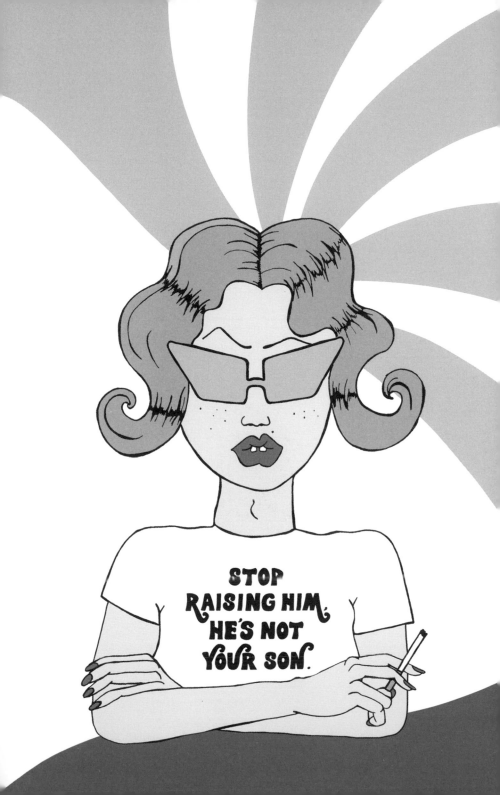

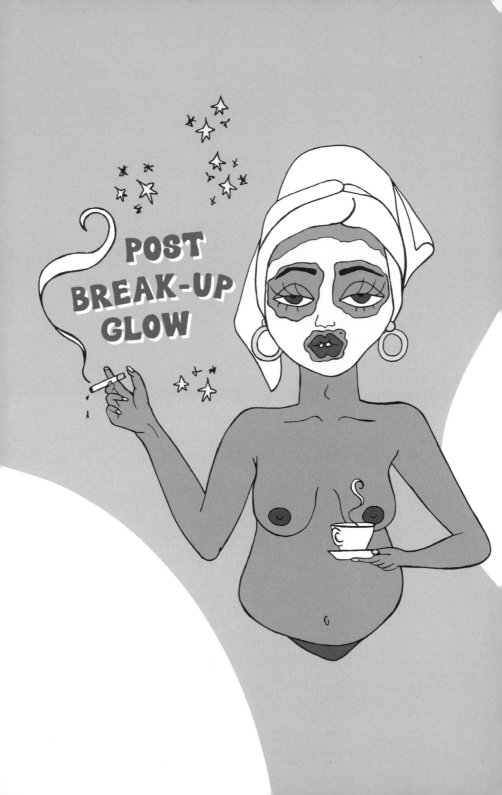

You are not his mum.
You are not his therapist.
You do not owe anyone that energy.
You owe that shit to *yourself*.

Want to know what the final straw with my ex was that finally made me dump him? He called me a *bitch*. Much worse had happened in our relationship, but in that moment something just clicked. I realized that if my unconscious self-neglect had reached the point where this behaviour had become so normalized, that someone close in my life had the audacity to comfortably and carelessly *call me a bitch* – I owed a lot of TLC and rehabilitation to myself. That word managed to penetrate the thick surface of the bubble I'd been living in for the last three years, and successfully burst it.

Don't ever value your relationship on how much shit you can take from someone. Heteronormativity, movies, novels, your parents and even your friends will have you believing that you're "strong" for "putting up with a man's shit". *Lord.* Can you hear it now? *Please* tell me you can hear how absurd this notion is! Your ability to take shit from a man and "stick by his side" says nothing about how strong you are. It does, however, say everything about your low self-esteem, and how much of a people-pleasing pushover this person has manipulated you into becoming. You have learned to betray yourself and compromise the things you desire and believe in, for the validation that you are desired by someone.

People who do not add any value to your life deserve no place in it. Simple. We waste so much of our time seeking validation from others, without realizing that everything we need already exists in ourselves. If you're lowering your standards to let someone into your life, dump them. Lowering your standards means that you're compromising your boundaries. Boundaries should never be compromised, they are your own personal law. Anyone who crosses them after you have explicitly addressed them has *broken* your law and needs to be banished from the access of knowing you. People will call you intimidating, bossy, make you believe that you have set your standards too high, and you might start to believe them. *Don't.* Your phone may be dry for a few months, you might not go on a successful date with someone for over a year, but honestly, who cares? Buy a sex toy! Wouldn't you rather spend that time focusing on your career, nurturing your mental health and preserving your beautiful energy? Rather than waste it on someone who makes you feel like you need to shrink yourself to make room for them in your life, in exchange for their crumbs? Ignoring red flags will only come back to bite you in the ass later!

You deserve better, and the annoying thing is that you already know this.

DATING RED FLAGS

Here are five signs that you're compromising yourself and your boundaries, and that you should DUMP THEM.

If you feel like you're compromising your politics by being with this person, dump them.

Trying to change someone's entire political belief system is far too much unpaid labour, and totally not worth it. There are nearly 8 billion people on this planet and no matter your sexuality, there's someone out there who holds the same beliefs as you. I know that sometimes it can feel like it's our responsibility to educate people (especially if they're a bigot) but it is not your responsibility to help "grow" or "change" this person. It's also impossible.

If you feel like you have to "tone down" or compromise your style for someone, dump them.

If any part of your identity at all is being squashed, suppressed or erased, they're not the one for you. There's someone out there who is so ready to love you and accept every gorgeous facet of your identity. (Hint: *it's you.*)

If you find that you're always withholding your good news from someone, or you feel like you need to undermine your achievements to make them comfortable when you do tell them good news, dump them.

Don't fuck with people who have such a fragile sense of self that your achievements make them uncomfortable. Good luck to them! I hope they heal their wounds, but it's not your job. Dump them.

If you have to say "no" more than once because they ignored you the first time, "didn't hear you" or coerced you into something you originally said you didn't want to do, dump them.

There are no blurred lines when it comes to enthusiastic consent. If they do not respect your boundaries, they do not respect you. This goes beyond sex. Someone who chooses to ignore you when you say "no" to anything is bad news.

If they make you feel like you need to shrink yourself, if they belittle your achievements, mock or attack the things you care about, dump them.

An ex of mine would constantly belittle my music taste, and I think he did it to assert power – making him feel in control of his own life. Now I get to dance around in my pants, uncompromised, to whatever the hell kind of music I want. Bliss.

If you find yourself constantly making up excuses for your partner's behaviour to your friends and family, or you lie about your partner's behaviour to your friends, dump them.
When we hide the details from people it's because we know we will have to be accountable and make changes.

Alternatively, if you find you yourself doing any of these to your partner or someone you're dating, then you're not ready for a relationship. You have a lot of stuff to work on and you are not ready to enter a reciprocal and healthy relationship until those parts of yourself are healed, either through therapy or deep self-reflection. You must not seek wholeness and validation in others and relationships; it's unfair for them to take on the labour of fixing you and be at the receiving end of emotional abuse.

Stop putting up with things you don't have to put up with. Surround yourself only with things that make you happy – everything else must go. What is a relationship's purpose in your life, if it does not bring you joy?

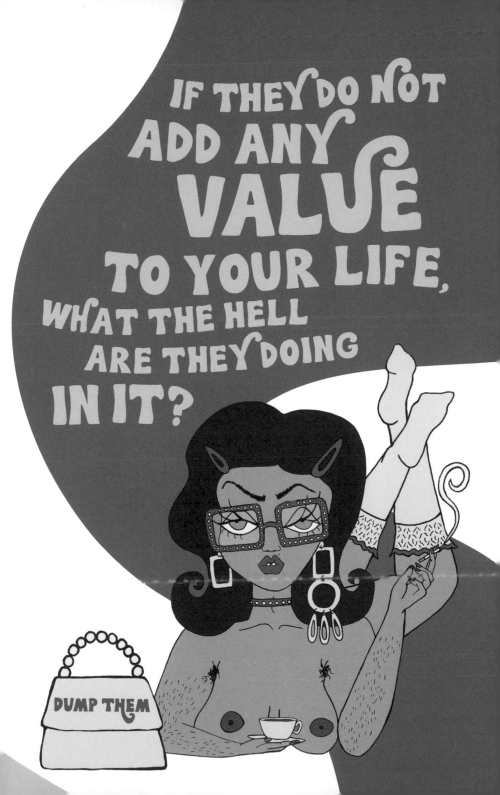

CHAPTER 17

YOU DON'T HAVE TO GET MARRIED

(NO, *REALLY*)

I am not against marriage. But...

I am all for people doing whatever the hell they want as long as it doesn't harm someone in the process. And, if that happens to involve getting married then I'm happy for those who choose to walk down that aisle. However, no matter how hard the world has tried, the institution of marriage has never been something I've felt I needed to complete my life for the following reasons:

- Imagine getting the government involved once you've fallen in love with someone to make sure they don't leave?
- Imagine also needing permission from the government to leave that relationship?
- Imagine having to ask your father's permission for you to be owned by someone else?
- Imagine your father "giving you away", as you pass down the aisle – like cattle, from one owner to the next, ready to be branded with a new surname?

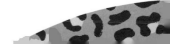

- Imagine your father viewing this exchange as a beautiful tradition, and one of his "life-long goals"?
- Imagine feeling like you have to stay with someone because you are contracted to stay with them, for the rest of your life?
- Imagine partaking in a ceremony that has historically excluded LGBTQ+ people and interracial relationships?
- Imagine being trans, and your wife/husband/partner being able to legally veto your right to transition?

Marriage is deeply entrenched in archaic patriarchal tradition and has its roots in an abusive, oppressive history – the ownership of women.

Heteronormativity has truly fucked us all up so much, to the point that we have widely accepted marriage as the pinnacle of great romance (so much so that we feel offended when our partner takes "too long" to propose!). The point of marriage has always been to own women and their bodies. Until 1991 you could legally rape your wife in the UK. Once she uttered the words "I do" at the altar, it meant that you could do what you pleased with her, because with the permission of her father she was now *your* property, and no longer his. The rape of an unmarried woman used to be viewed as a property crime against her father, robbing him of his daughter's virginity. In some cases the woman was forced to marry her rapist. The rape of a married woman by a man other than her husband was construed as a crime against her husband, with no concern for the woman herself. Marriage was (and still is in some countries) seen as a contract of ownership.

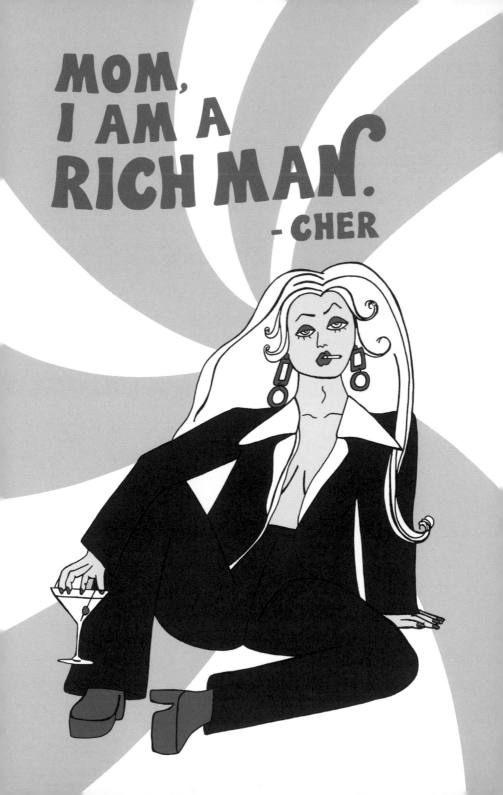

THE "SECOND SHIFT"

When working women in heterosexual marriages come home from their jobs – *they prepare for their second shift.*

Household contributions, always being someone's emotional support system, putting everyone before ourselves – acknowledging this as *real labour* explains why I have felt so exhausted in past relationships, and has liberated me and enabled me to set boundaries around my emotional intelligence and abundant empathy, something I used to give so freely to everyone but myself.

"Women are just better at that stuff!"

Women's unpaid contributions to the wellbeing of their homes, partners and children are overlooked, and put down to the fact that women are just natural-born caregivers. We are socialized to be more in touch with our emotions, and we are then expected to be caregivers because of it.

The antiquated gender roles of our society still expect women to do the majority of domestic work in the house and with our partners. Society hasn't yet caught up with the fact that most of us are now also working full-time jobs. As a result, women everywhere are fucking exhausted! We don't ever switch off. But because the impact of household labour isn't tangible, and you can't showcase how much it helps so many people, we are rarely rewarded or compensated for our time and energy. It becomes expected rather than gratefully accepted. In fact, a lot of narratives about married women praise them for self-sacrifice, and their ability to "give everything up" for love and "stick by their man through everything". How often do you hear that used in narratives about men?

Married heterosexual men rarely need to "make time for themselves" because they have built-in self-care: their wives.

I often think about what would happen if, for just one day, women everywhere refused to over-extend themselves. I truly believe the world as we know it would crumble. Remembering people's birthdays, ironing and cleaning clothes, anticipating others' needs, cooking, tidying up after others, being polite and smiling at men who make us uncomfortable, doing our make-up in the mornings and skincare routine before bed, booking doctor and dentist appointments for others and nagging them to be on time, offering our help without any real acknowledgement for it. Women are often in positions where they have to constantly remind men to take care of themselves, neglecting themselves in the process. *This is why self-care is uniquely important for women and marginalized genders.*

At the time of writing, I am 21 years old and have only been in one long-term relationship with a man. I lived with him for a month and, despite not being married, I found myself slipping into the role of *housewife*. He'd return from work and I'd ask him to pick up his things that he'd spewed across the floor, and he'd say, "I've been at work all day, I'm exhausted" as if I hadn't been working all day too. Delegating chores was non-existent, it was an act of labour even *asking* him to help out. One day he came home, opened the cupboards and said, "Why is there no food? I'm hungry." It was then that I realized I had become his carer, not his girlfriend.

THE NARRATIVE™

We have been indoctrinated over the centuries to romanticize weddings, and society distracts women from the oppressive truth using the usual persuasive capitalist methods, only this time with the illusory haze of an engagement ring and the promise that once we are married we will finally be living our perfect life. It is only when we choose to live by The Narrative™ (aka husband, house, kids) that we will feel complete and that we have succeeded because we have achieved all of life's goals. *Or so we're told.* First there is the beautiful ceremony where the bride is encouraged to spend up to a year "perfecting" her image to become the object of her husband's desire, while choosing the perfect white dress.

As most of us have spent our lives absorbing the message that women must be desirable objects for men, spending up to a year perfecting our image to become the ideal bride isn't *too* far from our everyday reality of performing femininity and desirability to receive a basic level of respect. I think it's important to acknowledge that for some people *not* getting married isn't an option. People marry for all sorts of reasons outside of love; it's also been a long-fought battle for LGBT people to have their relationship recognized, and for some trans people being able to participate in marriage provides a semblance of safety and "normalcy". We can't ignore that society rewards us with certain privileges the closer to this narrative we get. Aside from not having your life decisions questioned constantly, being married rewards you with significant tax and pension perks too.

A woman is so much more than her relationship status. It's literally the least interesting thing about her. Something I've practised doing with my friends as an attempt to reverse years of heteronormative brainwashing, is to refrain from asking them about their love life when we are having a catch up. If they bring it up, they bring it up. But by immediately asking our friends "Sooooo are you seeing anyone at the moment? Tell me all the details!", we emphasize the importance of romantic relationships in our lives, and reinforce that we are defined by our relationship status. What if they're not seeing anyone, will you be just as excited for them then? Ask them about what they've been up to instead, how their job's going or if they have any exciting projects coming up. If we want people to live happy and fulfilled lives regardless of their relationship status, we can start by deprioritizing the topic of our love lives in our conversations.

Ask yourself if marriage is something you've "always wanted to do".

Or if it's something you've always been *told* you wanted to do.

CHAPTER 18

STOP ASSUMING

To assume makes an ass of you and me.
Don't assume someone's ethnicity.
Don't assume someone's ability.
Don't assume someone's gender.
Don't assume someone's sexuality.
Don't assume someone's pronouns.
Don't assume someone's background.
Don't assume shit.
Full stop.

GENDER

It's in our nature to assume things of people. We pick up certain pieces of information from their appearance and body language and make a quick assessment based on how they present themselves and how they act around us. It helps us to understand things. But we must learn to take these identity indicators as just that. *A first assessment*.

We're raised from birth to exist within binaries – male or female, blue or pink – and each has their own rigid, archaic gender roles associated. Most of us accept this socially constructed narrative as *fact*, because there are birth certificates and institutions that were created to legitimize it, shaming anyone who dares to exist outside of this narrative, putting their lives in danger.

While a lot of people like myself are privileged to identify with the gender they were assigned at birth, unsurprisingly, a lot of people do not. It doesn't mean there's anything wrong with them, As described by activist and spoken-word poet Alok Vaid-Menon, "I wasn't born in the wrong body. I was born in the wrong *world*." A world that pre-determines every detail of your life and how it will look, right down to the colour of your clothing. And this is before you've even exited the womb, based on the way your genitals formed in utero. Bonkers, right?

Gender is entirely different to sex. *Sex* typically refers to genitalia – the biological differences between "male" and "female" bodies. Your *gender* is how you choose to identify, your perception of yourself and how you feel you identify within our society's ideas of gender. Gender exists on a spectrum, meaning that if you don't feel you identify with male or female, you might choose to adopt the label "non-binary" or "gender-fluid", and use gender-neutral pronouns such as they/them. Gender is not a fixed, half-pink half-blue two-dimensional shape. Just like sexuality, it exists on a glorious multi-dimensional spectrum, and cannot be assumed based on someone's genitals, or the colour of their clothing.

Gender expression, gender identity and sexuality are not intrinsically linked.

I identify as a woman, the gender I was assigned at birth. So I am a cisgender woman. This is my *gender identity*.

The way I dress, how I do my hair and make-up and present my gender, is my *gender expression*.

I have the capacity to date people of all genders, I identify as queer and this is my *sexuality*. None of these affects the others.

However, my *sexuality* is constantly *assumed* to be straight because my *gender expression* is very feminine and by default we assume that femininity is performed exclusively for men.

If people stopped assuming that I was straight and instead had an open mind, it might mean that I wouldn't have to constantly come out to people – *every single day*.

Just because a cisgender man wears a pink dress, it does not automatically mean that he's transgender, or that he's gay. He's just a man who likes to wear pink dresses. Colours don't have a gender. *We placed gender onto them*, because gender was socially constructed, it is an idea. Clothes merely communicate connotations and assumptions about these *ideas* of gender.

No matter how liberal your household was when you were growing up, it's impossible to escape the gender binary and heteronormative ways of living. It has penetrated every facet of our lives. But there are ways that we can consciously rewrite this narrative and reduce the impact it has on our lives, and the lives of people after us. It's time to change the narrative, and we can start with our language.

Every single day we assume people's gender. We don't even realize we're doing it because heteronormative culture runs so deep it has become instinctual. We are *obsessed* with gender. Do you freak out when you see a newborn baby because you don't know whether to say, "he's adorable!" or "she's adorable!" at the risk of getting it wrong? Just say, "they're adorable!". It's really that simple. Gender isn't binary (male or female), and using gender-neutral pronouns shows consideration. It shows that you haven't *assumed*.

FEMALE ARTIST

There are certain "defaults" in our society, usually reverting back to whiteness, sexist gender roles and heterosexuality. I am constantly referred to as a "female artist" or "female illustrator", and my friends who are in bands are referred to as "female musicians". Which at first glance, wouldn't seem offensive to most people. But words hold so much power, and what

WE CAN'T GIVE A ONE-SIZE-FITS-ALL NARRATIVE TO BILLIONS OF PEOPLE, AND EXPECT IT TO FIT EVERY SINGLE ONE OF THEM.

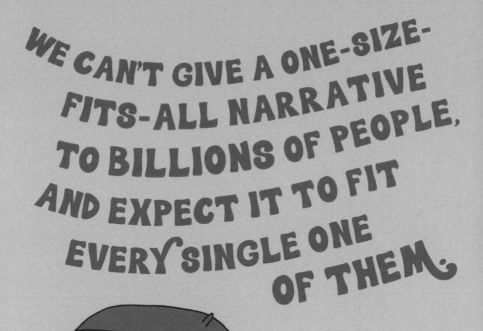

TRANS PEOPLE **EXIST.** DEAL WITH IT.

JUST BECAUSE
WE CAN EXPLAIN
SOMEONE'S
BEHAVIOUR
THAT DOES NOT MEAN
WE EXCUSE IT.

this implies is that artists, musicians and illustrators are inherently *male*. You would never hear anyone say "male artist". The same default bias is highlighted when the characters we read about in books and *assume* to be white are, to our surprise, portrayed by a person of colour in the movie. Whiteness is so default that only recently were there ballet shoes and flesh-coloured plasters produced in varying skin tones. My landlord told me someone was coming over to check the gas, and I was (pleasantly) surprised when a woman showed up at my door. When you come across yourself assuming these defaults, try to catch yourself in that moment and remember that these stereotypes are a powerful tool of oppression, because they are the limiting narratives that we tell oppressed people to keep them "in their place".

MIND YOUR BIAS

All of us have bias filters and they vary, depending on our upbringing, experiences and the narratives we absorb about ourselves and others in the media. We mostly operate from the subconscious part of our minds, and the stereotypes we absorb about people can impact our behaviour towards them without us even realizing, resulting in microaggressions.

Here are some examples of microaggressions:
- Crossing the street when you see a Black man.
- Asking people of colour, "But where are you *really* from?".
- Asking gay couples, "Which one's the man and which one's the woman?"
- White women saying, "Hey guuuurl" and snapping their fingers at their Black girl friends, when they would never do this with their white counterparts.
- Telling a person of colour that they are "so articulate".
- Using disablist slurs such as "ret*rd" or "crazy".

- Asking a woman about her "boyfriend/husband" when she has only ever referred to a "partner".
- "She's trans? Wow I would have had no idea, she looks like a *real* woman."
- Trying to set up a gay person you meet with "your other gay friend".
- Clutching your purse tighter when you see a Black person on the street.
- Saying that Black hair is "unprofessional" for the workplace, asking questions about Black hair, vocalizing opinions on Black hair, or asking to touch Black hair.
- Men interrupting women when they're talking in meetings with "Well actually, I think..."
- Asking women what they were wearing when they recount experiences of sexual harassment or assault.
- Calling women of colour "exotic".
- Men saying, "You're not like other girls" (or women saying, "I'm not like other girls").
- Hosting panel discussions, events and exhibitions with all-white participants, artists or speakers.
- Calling neighbourhoods "dodgy", when they just predominantly consist of Black and minority ethnic people
- Singing the N-word in songs (you'd think us non-Black folks would have caught onto this by now, but I'm putting it here just in case).

The difference between microaggressions like these and overt racism/sexism/homophobia is that microaggressions are unintentional.

We don't know in our *conscious* mind that we are "othering" this person based on our *subconscious* beliefs about them, which were formed from years of socialization.

While this explains our behaviour, it does not *excuse it*. When people call us out on these behaviours, our priority should always be to make sure that the person we've hurt is okay. Whether you intended to hurt them or not, the truth is that you did. The impact of your actions is always more important than your intentions if you have caused someone harm. The next chapter focuses on accountability and apologizing.

So. Listen to people who have experiences outside of your own, stop assuming people's sexuality and always ask for someone's pronouns if you're unsure.

Got it?

CHAPTER 19

ACCOUNTABILITY

When the people in your life pull you up on your behaviour or encourage you to be held accountable, it is an act of love.

It might feel like a personal attack initially, but if someone cares enough to tell you that something you have said has hurt them, that's them making an effort to preserve your relationship. They value you and they want you to understand the impact of your words so that it doesn't happen again. Equally, holding yourself accountable for your actions is *self*-love. This is how we grow.

If you're going to leave room for growth and form meaningful connections in your life, it's necessary to get over your need to be right all the time.

Phrases to avoid when apologizing:
- "I'm sorry *you feel* this way, but..."
- "I think you've taken this the wrong way."
- "I think you're overreacting."
- "I didn't mean it like that."
- "I don't think that's fair because..."

This is a reaction. Not a response.

A response is carefully formulated after you have processed what has been said and had time to empathize with the perspective offered up to you. A response includes self-reflection, it involves you looking inwards.

It doesn't matter what you meant, or what your intentions were. What matters is the impact of your actions, and that they have harmed someone. *Someone is hurt!* Your priority should be rectifying the situation and reducing the damage to make this person feel as safe as possible. The best lesson I ever learned was to work on getting out of the habit of reacting, and start responding instead. When someone calls you out on your behaviour, your initial reaction might be to defend yourself, because you can't for a second imagine that you are capable of hurting someone, especially if it was unintentional.

But if someone is hurt, they want an apology – not an excuse.

Sure, if you feel it's necessary you can explain your side of things, but verbally acknowledge that while this *explains* your behaviour it does not *excuse* it. It does not excuse that someone is hurt.

HOW TO RESPOND

Let's say your friend has confronted you about how they feel you've been ignoring them lately. They say that you've been spending a lot of time with your new partner, that they're delighted for you because your happiness means everything to them, *but* your new relationship has made them feel shut out. How should you process this and make sure you're responding rather than reacting?

Apologize

It doesn't matter that you didn't mean to make them feel that way, the fact is that they *do* feel that way, and their feelings are *valid*. Tell them this. Let them know that you have acknowledged their feelings and that you are sorry.

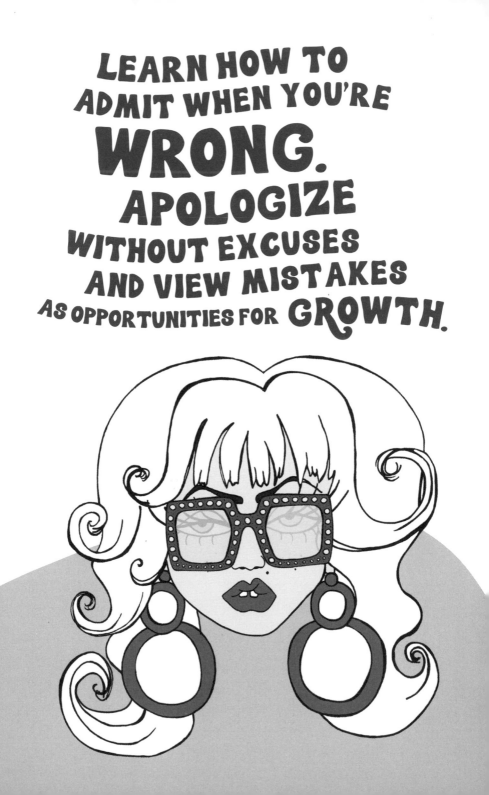

"I'm so sorry I have caused you to feel this way, you didn't deserve to feel like that."

"Your feelings are entirely valid."

"Thank you for sharing this with me, it means a lot that you felt comfortable to talk to me about this."

You might feel angry

Your initial defence response might be that you think they're "jealous" – but if you feel angry or you feel the need to defend and excuse why you did what you did, *stop right there.* The best thing to do in this situation is to give yourself time to cool down and self-reflect. When we become defensive, we put ourselves at the centre of the situation – and this isn't about you, it's about your friend and making sure they feel safe and comfortable to talk to you about their feelings. When we become defensive and say things like "you're overreacting!" or "you're just jealous" we cause the person to doubt their feelings and foster a hostile environment. It's a form of emotional gaslighting. This person won't feel comfortable vocalizing their feelings to you again, and if this cycle repeats itself enough times it forms the foundation of an emotionally abusive relationship. If someone feels they can't speak up in a relationship, it's abusive.

Acknowledge that you may have overlooked their needs

You might have prioritized your new relationship over your friendship, and that's okay, it happens! But your friend is hurt. Even though this wasn't your intention, you must acknowledge this has made them feel upset and that you want to come to a solution. Ask what this means for them, and what actions they feel are necessary to rectify the situation. Or if you can think of something, suggest yourself! Maybe ask them if they'd like to schedule a day of the month that's blocked off just for you two to have coffee together? There's nothing better than having your feelings acknowledged by someone who also pro-actively tries to find a solution to make you feel better. Be actively engaged in reaching a solution.

Come back with correct behaviour

Apologies without changed behaviour are insincere. They are also a form of emotional manipulation! What can you do moving forward to make sure that you don't encounter this situation again?

Having a conversation like this requires both people to put aside their egos and talk directly to one another to find a solution. If this kind of straightforward communication is hard for you, try writing an email or a text instead. Direct and face-to-face conversations can be overwhelming for people who struggle with anxiety and other mental illnesses, but there are always other ways to be held accountable and resolve conflict that don't require this level of stress. I find that texts and emails work better for me personally, usually followed up with a phone call to get more of a back and forth about how we can find a solution. It can be hard to understand someone's tone through text, leading to further miscommunication. So building a conversation can be a useful and effective means to a quicker and more sustainable resolution.

HOLDING SOMEONE ELSE ACCOUNTABLE

Setting and holding boundaries is a way to filter out the people who simply don't matter. How a person responds to my boundaries, or how they respond to me telling them that they have done something hurtful, helps me decide whether or not I should keep them around.

IF PEOPLE CAN'T
BE ACCOUNTABLE
OR APOLOGIZE
FOR HURTING SOMEONE
- WHETHER THEY MEANT
TO OR NOT -
IT'S A RED FLAG.

NO
IT'S THE RED FLAG.

If someone can't put aside their ego to consider someone else's perspective, realize that they exist outside of their own perception and that *gasp* they are in fact human and they made a mistake, they are not the kind of person you want in your life. I have been told that I'm too strict with my boundaries, that I need to loosen them up a little, and I have been called a "bitch" for saying what I do and don't want. The people who told me that are no longer in my life. Because what people really mean by this, is that my readiness to implement boundaries reminds them that they might not have such fiercely guarded boundaries in place in their own lives. What they're also asking me to do is compromise myself. Compromise? *For what!* Why should I change and bend my boundaries for people when the reason they're there in the first place is to protect myself from things I know, from experience, will cause me harm? Boundaries are intentional, you have them for a reason. If someone refuses to respect them they are violating and breaking your personal law.

Red-flag responses when you try to hold someone accountable:

- You feel the need to back down from your initial statement, or change it to make it more palatable, because they got defensive.
- Their reaction makes you feel the need to apologize for not "saying it nicely". Remember, *they're the person who owes an apology.*
- You feel as though you are treading on eggshells because they got defensive when you confronted them, you're worried about saying the wrong thing and what they might do.
- They go to great lengths to explain why they did what they did, their thought process behind it and so on, instead of just acknowledging that you're hurt and that they're responsible.
- They turn themselves into the victim and start talking about what they're going through.
- They refuse to apologize.

- They say they "don't feel like they have anything to apologize for".
- They shame you into self-reflection, making you feel "too much" for setting your boundary.
- They put you in a position where you're having to coddle and look after them (tears, getting upset, using their mental illness or trauma to excuse why they hurt you).

Equally, if you have ever exhibited any of these behaviours yourself, now is a good time to reflect and examine why these feelings came up for you, and why you felt the need to defend yourself in this way. It's okay, we all fuck up. But you might owe someone an apology.

If someone becomes defensive and goes to great lengths to let me know their entire thought process as to *why* they did what they did, tells me I could have said it "a different way" or even refuses to say sorry because they "haven't done anything wrong" – they will not be hearing from me again. At least, not until they recognize what they have done. Even then, you do not owe anyone your forgiveness.

You will never receive an apology from someone who refuses to see your perspective because they will always believe that they've done nothing wrong.

Forget it.

You tried.

Move on.

Focus on your healing.

Their karma is being who they are.

CHAPTER 20

CHECK YOUR PRIVILEGE

What does privilege really mean?

To have privilege is to be afforded unearned benefits in society, based on being part of a social group. E.g. White men are able to walk around at night safely without fear of street harassment, rape or murder.

It's possible to be both oppressed and privileged at the same time. E.g. I'm a queer woman and face oppression from homophobia and sexism, but I am also extremely privileged in that I am white, thin, non-disabled, cisgender and neurotypical so I am afforded more opportunities at the expense of people who don't have these privileges.

We are far more likely to be aware of our negative experiences of oppression rather than ways in which we are privileged, because our privileges are actually just fair treatment that *everyone* should be entitled to. We assume it's how everyone else is treated, because it's our reality and it feels "normal". Privilege is invisible to the person who has it until it's pointed out to them, or after they have lost that privilege. E.g. I didn't realize what a privilege it was just to be able to show public displays of affection until I began dating women, when I'd fear for our safety just by holding hands in public.

The thing about privilege, is that it can't exist without oppression.

The reason you are privileged is because another group is suffering and paying for it. Ever wondered why people cause such a fuss over white girls in cornrows and braids? Because the act of being able to "dip into" Black culture and not face the struggles that they do when they perform their own culture, is rooted in an unspeakable amount of privilege. Black women are told their hair is "ghetto" in cornrows, "unprofessional" when they wear it natural, and Black kids are sent home from school for wearing out their natural hair as it's "too distracting". It's a privilege to be able to waver in and out of Black culture – but not actually have to go through the same struggles and obstacles that these groups face – as a person who benefits from their oppression. Exercising your privilege in this way is harmful and offensive, and until Black people can live their lives without being punished for their hair, white people in dreadlocks will never be "just a hairstyle". It will always be political.

Peggy McIntosh describes white privilege as "an invisible package of unearned assets that I can count on cashing in each day, but about which I was 'meant' to remain oblivious. White privilege is like an invisible weightless knapsack of special provisions, maps, passports, codebooks, visas, clothes, tools, and blank checks."

A white person can be oppressed for a number of reasons, but never because they're white. Having privilege does not mean that you haven't had a hard life or worked hard to get to where you are. It just means that someone else in your position without your privileges faces a lot more obstacles to be in that spot, let alone the obstacles they faced getting there in the first place. E.g. A white person living in poverty still has white privilege, because being Black and poor is harder.

Here are some privilege checklists to help you recognize where you might have been given a leg-up in society.*

* Boise State Writing Center, https://sites.google.com/a/u.boisestate.edu/social-justice-training/about-us/our-training/privilege-checklist

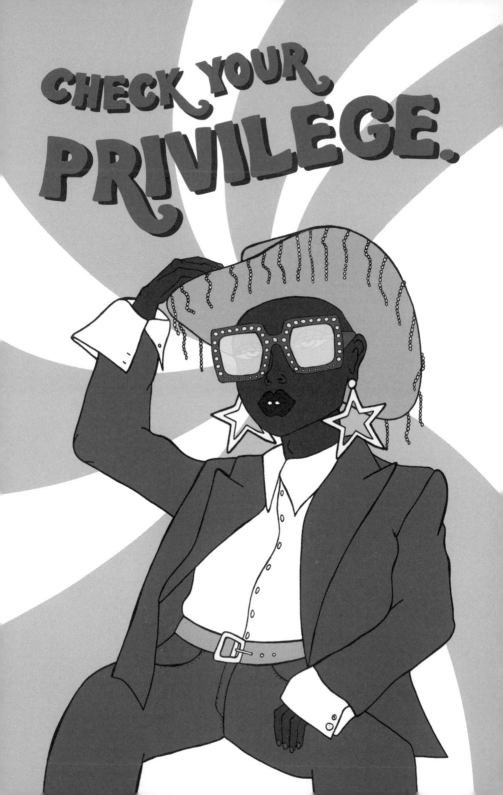

White race, ethnicity and culture privilege

☐ People know how to pronounce my name.

☐ I am never mocked or perceived as a threat because of my name.

☐ I know that the police are there to protect me and I don't feel threatened by their presence.

☐ People of my race are widely represented in media.

☐ I don't ever have to think about my race or ethnicity.

☐ I don't really think about race at all.

☐ I do not have to worry about imprisonment unless I commit a serious crime.

☐ I can choose plasters in flesh colour and have them more or less match my skin.

☐ My ethnicity will not make people around me uncomfortable.

☐ I can go to the shop knowing that no one will be suspicious of me.

☐ I don't have to check whether my ethnicity will cause problems when choosing travel destinations.

Cisgender privilege

- ☐ I can use public facilities like restrooms and locker rooms without fear of verbal abuse, assault or arrest.

- ☐ People know what to call me and how to refer to me without asking first.

- ☐ I do not have to worry that my gender expression will make people around me uncomfortable.

- ☐ Strangers don't ask me what my genitals look like and how I have sex.

- ☐ I have the ability to walk through the world and blend in, without being whispered about, pointed at or laughed at because of my gender expression.

- ☐ If I end up in the emergency room, I do not have to worry that my gender will keep me from receiving appropriate treatment, or that all of my medical issues will be seen as a result of my gender.

- ☐ I am able to purchase clothes that I like without being refused service/mocked by staff and questioned about my genitals.

- ☐ My gender is an option on all forms I have to fill in.

- ☐ I am legally recognized as a gender.

- ☐ I know that I can date someone and that they aren't just looking to satisfy a curiosity or kink pertaining to my gender identity.

Male/male passing privilege

☐ I can express myself, set boundaries and be assertive without being called a "bitch" or someone attributing it to "my time of the month".

☐ I can mess something up without it being seen as an indictment of my entire gender.

☐ I can walk the streets and enter public spaces without the threat of sexual harassment.

☐ At work, I don't often have to worry about harassment from customers, coworkers or bosses.

☐ I generally feel comfortable going somewhere alone at whatever time.

☐ I feel comfortable going on a date with someone new as I don't have to fear violence (straight men)

☐ I don't have to worry about people perceiving me as sexual because of my clothes or body.

☐ People do not often make unsolicited comments about my body.

☐ I am not expected to spend a great deal of time and money on my appearance.

☐ I'm not shamed when I choose *not* to spend my time and money on my appearance.

☐ I do not often have to fear sexual violence.

☐ When I speak up, my opinions are heard and respected equally with other people's.

☐ I am not diminished or treated differently because of my gender.

PRIVILEGE
IS USUALLY INVISIBLE
TO THE PERSON
WHO HAS IT
UNTIL IT'S POINTED
OUT TO THEM,
OR AFTER THEY HAVE
LOST THAT
PRIVILEGE.

Straight privilege

☐ I will receive public recognition/support for a romantic relationship.

☐ I feel comfortable displaying affection in public with my partner and don't expect hostile or violent reactions from others.

☐ I don't have to check that my sexuality is legal when choosing travel destinations with my partner.

☐ I can openly live with my partner.

☐ I can safely and comfortably hold hands with my partner in public.

☐ I have never had to hide or reveal my sexuality.

☐ I have never had to "come out" of binary sexuality assumptions or publicly speak about my sexuality with relative strangers.

☐ I have never experienced discrimination at work for my sexuality.

☐ I can learn about sex and relationships from movies and television.

☐ I have access to role models of my sexual orientation and accurate representation of people with whom I can identify.

☐ I can assume I am around others of my sexuality most of the time, and don't have to worry about being the only one of my sexuality in a class, job, or in a social situation.

☐ I can talk about my relationship without fearing judgement or violence.

☐ I can easily find a neighbourhood in which people will accept me.

☐ If I raise, adopt, or teach children, no one will assume that I will somehow force them into my sexuality.

☐ Strangers don't ask me how I have sex or how I could have children.

☐ I will not be mistreated by the police or people in authority because of my sexuality.

Non-disabled privilege

☐ I can go to new places knowing that I will be able to move through the space with ease and without pre-planning.

☐ I do not have to worry about making the people around me uncomfortable because of my disability.

☐ People do not treat me in an un-adult fashion by crouching down to me, using a patronizing tone or offering unsolicited help for tasks.

☐ I can succeed in situations without other people being surprised by that success or using the word "despite".

☐ My success is not presented as a guilt trip for others who do not have my disability. ("If they can do it despite their disability, what's your excuse?")

☐ I can go to any class, job or website and assume that the materials presented to me will be understandable.

☐ People don't think I'm lazy or stupid when I need to try something again or ask something to be made clearer.

☐ I am able to enter new situations without fear of debilitating anxiety, embarrassment, harassment or violence.

☐ No one assumes that any partner attracted to me must be a predator or paedophile, even though I am an adult.

Class/Financial Privilege

- ☐ I have access to transport that will get me where I need to go.

- ☐ I have knowledge of and access to community resources.

- ☐ I can swear or commit a crime without people attributing it to the low morals of my class.

- ☐ I can update my wardrobe with new clothes to match current styles and trends.

- ☐ People do not assume that I am unintelligent or lazy based on the dialect I grew up speaking.

- ☐ Regardless of the season, I can count on my home remaining a comfortable temperature.

- ☐ I know that I will be able to go to the supermarket when I need to and will be able to buy the healthy foods that I want.

- ☐ Whenever I've moved out of my home it has been voluntary, and I had another home to move into.

- ☐ I can plan on getting a raise at my job.

- ☐ My decision to go or not to go to college wasn't based entirely on financial determinants.

Privilege works in systems and institutions of power. People with institutional power are those who write the narratives – the CEOs of large companies (there are more CEOs named John than there are female CEOs altogether) and the people who dominate political conversation and present the political world to us. These people can use their positions to benefit themselves and other privileged people. If you are oppressed, you do not have this institutional power because your race/class/gender is simply not represented in enough of the people in these systems of power. Black people do not have racial institutional power, women do not have gender-based institutional power. Therefore, "reverse racism" and "female privilege" does not exist, because in order to cause oppression you need institutional power. Misandry (the hatred of men) has never led to job loss, rape, murder or mass oppression for men – the way that misogyny (the hatred of women) has for women. However, because we have multiple identities and are able to face both oppression and privilege at the same time, white women in power are still capable of holding up racism-based systems, and men of colour are capable of perpetuating and maintaining patriarchy.

We must look at the rule, and not the *exception* to the rule. So many times people will point at individuals such as Oprah Winfrey, or the fact America had a Black president, to prove that "racism is over". But privilege works as a system, and it goes round in a vicious cycle. Let's say a company is full of white cisgender men. They claim that they hire based on "qualifications" and that they "don't discriminate". Even if this *were* true, the reason people of colour are less likely to have the same qualifications as their white counterparts is because of socio-economic factors that prevent them from getting the education they need in the first place, being a disenfranchised and oppressed group in society. Universities are less likely to accept Black students because of racial bias. Even when they are accepted, Black students are more likely to fail their class and not graduate because of lack of support in their studies. A white man with a criminal record has a higher chance of receiving a job offer than a Black man with a *clean record.*[*]

Read that shit again.

---

[*] Devah Pager, *Marked: Race, Crime, and Finding Work in an Era of Mass Incarceration* (Chicago: University of Chicago Press, 2009).

All of the little microaggressions and instances of racism that filter through our society are what keeps the cycle of oppression in motion, maintaining the status quo that keeps privileged people at the top.

It's crucial that we are aware of how nothing in our lives is untouched by our privilege. The point of being cognizant of our privileges is not to engender feelings of guilt – guilt is pointless and does nothing for feminism or activating social change.

Being aware of your privilege allows you to spend it to benefit other people. As you move through the world, think of the opportunities you could pass on or how you could give up space for people who don't have the same access to important spaces that you do. Real change happens when we give up power, without telling anyone we did it.

Are you hiring people for a new project? Make sure that there are people of colour on board. Have you been asked to speak on an all-white panel? Decline the invite, tell them why and suggest they hire a greater diversity of people who would open up the narrative and be able to voice another perspective. Can you see a woman or a visibly queer person being harassed on the street? Walk with them, make sure they feel safe and intervene. The only way to break these cycles and create a world where people are treated equally is to challenge it. Not by "waiting for the racists and misogynists to die out".

Because they're still inside all of us. We need to fight them from within.

CHAPTER 21

LET THAT SHIT GO

There will never be a point in your life when you're entirely "healed". But whether it's a break up or something more traumatic – shit gets *better*.

There are parts of myself that I have lost to traumatic events, and I'm not sure if I will ever get them back. Accepting that I will never be the same despite how unfair these events have been has helped me to move through them, rather than be destroyed by them. I learned the important and hard truth that my healing process is *my* responsibility and no one else's. The same way you cannot fix other people, no one else can heal and fix you. It's unfair because you didn't deserve whatever happened to you, but there's no reason to find a "lesson" in your experience, nor to try to be the same person you were before it happened to you. Finding meaning in traumatic events should not be your priority; your priority should be trying to *survive*. I hate the phrase "everything happens for a reason" when used in the context of trauma, because sometimes terrible things happen to really incredible people and they don't deserve it, but they *have to* find and fight a way through. If your healing process is contingent on validation from other people, or an apology, you will never be free of the control it exerts over you. Accepting this alone played an enormous part in the healing process that I'm still embarking on, every single day.

"ARE YOU HEALED OR ARE YOU JUST DISTRACTED?"*

In the past, I have utilized little coping mechanisms and pockets of joy that temporarily felt like glue, filling up the cracks caused by trauma and helping to make me feel whole again. This could be dating someone new, having a casual fling, ordering myself take-out, or spending money on skin-care products to make *the outside* feel better. But as long as we keep using things that afford us only temporary, transient relief for a much deeper and complex problem – and we keep reaching for the quick-fix coping mechanisms – we never fully heal. We need to stop relying on quick-fix solutions or insubstantial "glue" to fill our cracks, and instead allow the cracks to heal properly on their own, forming bonds with each other and making stronger ones through self-reflection and accountability. You cannot heal by using external factors and validation. It has to come from within.

At our lowest points, we tend to reach for things that can quickly and effectively "fill the void" or temporarily relieve our sense of it. Some use mind-altering substances, others use dating apps or go shopping. The thing with short-term gratification, however beautiful and effective it feels in the moment, is that it is fleeting. If left unchecked and not regulated, it often results in long-term self-destructive behaviours which end up prolonging our suffering, making us weaker and less able to take care of ourselves. Self-sabotage could be anything from binge-drinking or binge-eating, to checking up religiously on your ex's Instagram account, or frequenting the same places as the person who ghosted you in the hope you "bump into them". You might not even realize you're doing it, but all are acts of self-sabotage and will prevent you from getting out of the position of needing an external factor to help you survive. To say "I'm healed" isn't the goal – the goal is to get out of the place in your head where you are an obstacle to your own progress.

* @Werenotreallystrangers

Finding the power to say "no" to things, people and habits that block my journey back to finding myself, has been the single most important act of self-care for me. In a world that encourages selflessness in women, and in which we are encouraged to be caregivers and nurturers, it seems we have neglected ourselves in the process. Bouncing back from self-neglect will be sold back to you in ways that improve your appearance, as opposed to addressing your mental state and wellbeing. But years of self-neglect is best healed through deep introspection. It involves discomfort. It involves being willing to admit that everything you thought you knew about the world, people and yourself may be just what you told yourself, so that you could cope and stay in a comfortable, familiar state of suffering. These are called "limiting narratives", they are the stories we tell ourselves over and over again to justify why things might not be working out for us in life. The only way to escape this cyclical, insufferable hell is to examine our behaviours and ask ourselves what needs to change. What behaviours might you keep exhibiting to enable you to remain in a comfortable and familiar state of suffering?

**Don't be afraid. By questioning everything,
you can only become a more refined
version of your already incredible self.**

"YOU'VE CHANGED!"

Outgrowing other people as well as habits is part of the healing and changing process. If you want to grow, you're going to have to ditch that mate you've let stick around because you've "known them for years", despite the fact they have proven to you time and time again they only reach out when they want

I CAN'T WAIT FOR YOU TO MEET AND **FALL IN LOVE** WITH THE PERSON **THAT THE WORLD** HAS KEPT YOU FROM BECOMING.

something from you. Outgrowing people is unfortunately inevitable. What *is* avoidable and entirely within your power, though, is how you allow these people to make you feel about your growth, and whether or not you keep them around long enough to affect it. *The only person in control of your happiness is you – make changes if you need to.* People hate to see you get out of situations that kept you grounded and suffering with them – it reminds them of their own journey of growth that they have yet to embark on, especially if you bonded with this person over a shared trauma. This is a much more subtle and undetectable way of self-sabotaging your growth. You might cling to people who share a similar trauma to you, or hang around with the people who remind you of the version of yourself that existed when the trauma happened for comfort. You never grow in these connections, because the foundation of your relationship is built on mutual suffering. If one of you grows, the other can't connect to you anymore.

But there are people in the world who are aching to see you thrive and get out of your cycle. Outgrowing people and letting them go is an act of choosing your own happiness, and making room for people who deserve a place in your life.

As you make the decision to work on yourself, heal, grow, become autonomous, start saying "no" and stop people-pleasing, you may start hearing things like this:

- "You think you're so much better than everyone now."
- "You've changed!"
- "Sorry I'm not good enough for you anymore."
- "You used to be fun."
- "Everything's about boundaries, loosen up."

All of these are forms of emotional manipulation. Healing comes with your ability to let go. If they don't want to assist your growth or support your growth, dump them.

HOW I GOT TO KNOW MYSELF, FALL IN LOVE WITH MYSELF AND HEAL MYSELF

At its core, nurturing self-love can be ugly. It's not always face masks and selfies. For me it involved a lot of crying, isolation, setting boundaries, self-reflection and even dancing around my flat naked. Self-care looks different for everyone, but here's how I shed the shrunken version of myself that I had become, and the steps I took to grow into my new divine self:

- I cried my eyes out while sitting on the floor talking to myself in the mirror.
- I took myself out for lunch, on my own.
- I got myself into therapy.
- I grew out all of my body hair.
- I kept a hand-written diary recording how I felt on a day-to-day basis. If you find it hard to keep up with writing a diary, try making a Word document. Mine from 2019 alone was 60,000 words long!
- I danced naked around my flat to my favourite music, free of any kind of gaze but my own.
- I bought and read books.
- I invested in self-healing through reading the work of psychologists.
- I bought my first vibrator to reclaim my body (and give myself earth-shattering orgasms, of course).
- I stopped isolating myself – by telling my friends how I'd been feeling for the first time.
- I talked to and hyped myself up in front of the mirror on a daily basis.
- I cried and screamed into my pillow.

- I recorded videos talking to the camera for when I'm feeling low, as a cathartic release and to recognize my self-destructive patterns.
- I took hundreds of nudes, that to this day no one else has seen but myself.
- I hung up gorgeous prints in my flat to surround myself with visually stimulating things I love.
- I shouted "FUCK YOU" to get myself out of bed in the mornings when it was hard, as a way of giving up the power that trauma had over me and my daily routine.
- I bought house plants to look after, tend to and water daily. (On days when you feel undeserving, like the world doesn't need you, your plants need you. Perfect for recovering co-dependents!)
- I cried on Facetime to friends for hours.
- I bought cute lingerie as I wanted to look good for my *god damn self.*
- I started to say "NO" instead of worrying about people's reactions and stuck to my decisions, because I decided to stop people-pleasing and put up some boundaries.
- I overcame my FOMO and stayed at home.
- I avoided situations, events or people that would impact the progress I had been making to heal myself.

Some things do develop beyond discomfort and turn into diagnosable mental health problems, such as depression, PTSD and eating disorders. At this point simple self-care and self examination aren't enough, and external care is required. For this reason exactly, I go to therapy weekly! If you do need help you should confide in your friends or family. There are also organizations that provide safe places to talk online or over the phone if you don't feel comfortable or ready to share with people close in your life, or if they are the cause of your situation.

FOR PERSPECTIVE

Healing is hard. If you have a tricky time appreciating the journey you've been on and how incredible it is that you're alive, I want you to imagine all the past versions of yourself, standing right in front of you. This could be:

- The person who was bullied in high school.
- The person who cried themselves to sleep.
- The one who drunk-sobbed in the toilets on a night out.
- The one who went through something so traumatic they thought life was broken beyond repair.
- The one who almost gave up on life completely.

Imagine all of the past versions of yourself, standing right in front of you. They are all smiling, looking back at you. They are so proud of you.

Because you *beat* what they were going through. You beat the things that tried to kill and destroy them. Because of *your* strength, you are still here in this present moment, in spite of what happened to those past versions of yourself.

They are grateful – you got all of them through this to be where you are today – alive.

GLOSSARY

Accountability – taking responsibility for your actions, words and beliefs, especially those things that could cause harm such as perpetuating racist beliefs or acting in a disablist way.

Ageism – discriminating against somebody on the basis of their age.

Butch – a person who has traits that are stereotypically described as masculine. Although often used within the lesbian community, not all butch women are lesbians (and not all lesbians are butch).

Capitalism – a system focused on creating financial profit. Businesses, properties and industry are owned privately and are designed to create profit for those who own them.

Cisgender – a person who is the gender they were assigned at birth. If a person was described as a girl when they were born, and still identify as a girl later in life, they are cisgender. Essentially, "not trans".

Fatphobia – prejudice or discrimination against somebody because they are fat. This can include not providing suitable accommodations (e.g. only having narrow chairs with arms), judging somebody for what they wear ("she can't get away with a mini skirt!") or not hiring somebody because of judgements about their weight.

Femme – a person whose identity or gender presentation tends towards being feminine can be described as femme. In the trans community, people can describe themselves as femme without identifying as a woman.

Hetrifying – to be hetrified is to be bombarded by heteronormative narratives and messaging (coined by Florence Given).

Heteronormative – a state in which heterosexuality is considered to be the norm and other sexual orientations are downplayed, dismissed or criticized.

Internalized misogyny – a state in which women turn the hatred of women (misogyny) against themselves and other women and favour men, criticize themselves and believe negative gender stereotypes.

Intersectional feminism – the acknowledgement of how aspects of identity intersect with being female to create unique experiences of discrimination. Originally coined by Kimberlé Williams Crenshaw.

LGBTQ+ – lesbian, gay, bisexual, transgender, queer and +, which indicates that more sexualities and gender identities (e.g. such as intersex, aromantic, asexual, questioning) exist.

Male gaze – a state in which the world is viewed as a heterosexual man would view it.

Marginalized – to be treated less well because of a characteristic that is discriminated against.

Me Too – movement started by Tarana Burke, where people speak up about the sexual harassment they have received.

Misogyny – prejudice or discrimination against, or hatred of, women.

Non-disabled – a preferred term because "able-bodied" could include people with mental health problems or those who are learning disabled, creating confusion.

Oppression – treating people unfairly, particularly because of a characteristic they possess that puts them at risk of discrimination or prejudice.

Patriarchy – a society or community where men are in charge. This can be on a formal level, such as many churches, or informally, where misogyny takes place and men are more powerful, such as in an abusive heterosexual relationship.

Pretty – somebody who is femme or female and considered to be conventionally attractive. This is an example of privilege that rewards certain women for things outside of their control

Privilege – rights or advantages that people experience because they are not marginalized in society. White privilege, non-disabled privilege, thin privilege etc. benefit people who do not work for that advantage but receive it anyway.

Queer – a term for people who are LGBTQ+ who do not conform to the norms of heterosexuality or being cisgender. It can also be used as a verb to describe looking at something from a different point of view (e.g. "queering history").

Self-sabotage – to get in the way of what's best for yourself.

Street harassment – persecution, hassle, being followed or experiencing sexual harassment on the street.

Survivor – somebody who has survived sexual abuse, sexual assault or rape. Survivor is often considered to be a more empowering term than "victim", though some people prefer to say they are "thriving" rather than surviving

Trans – somebody whose gender identity does not match the gender they were assigned at birth.

ACKNOWLEDGEMENTS

In a world where the voices of marginalized people are intentionally silenced, mocked or ignored when speaking up on the very same issues that thin, cis, non-disabled white women like me are not only heard on, but *praised* for, I want to acknowledge that the sections in this book on my understanding of prettiness, desirability, privilege, unconscious bias and systems of oppression didn't just fall into my head. I wasn't taught any of this in school, either. I had to search for this understanding. I had to listen and I had to learn, *predominantly from Black women.* My understanding of these topics would not have been possible without the work of the following women, who I am dedicating this book to. Some I have the privilege of knowing in real life, some through the wonderful world of the internet, and some I met because of the internet. Thank you for choosing over and over again to unapologetically voice your thoughts, undeterred by other people's reactions:

MUNROE BERGDORF

CHIDERA EGGERUE

ASHLEIGH NICOLE TRIBBLE

LAYLA SAAD

RACHEL CARGLE

CHAR ELLESSE

RENI EDDO-LODGE

AFRICA BROOKE

RACHEL RICKETTS

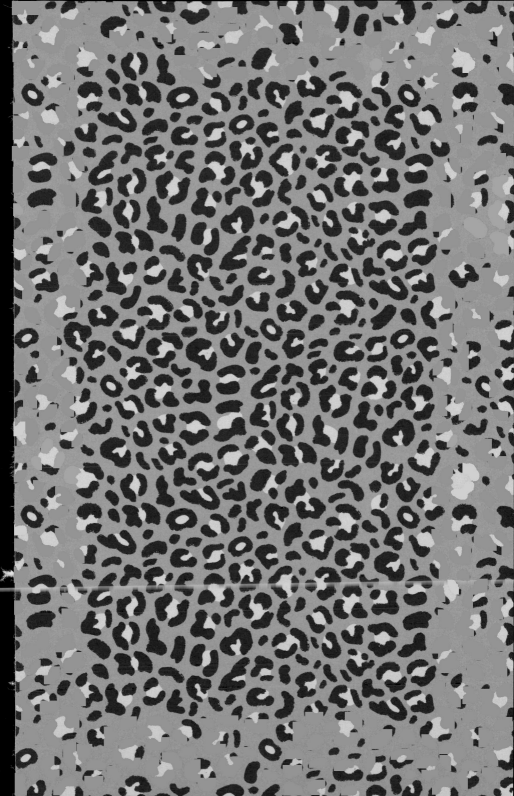

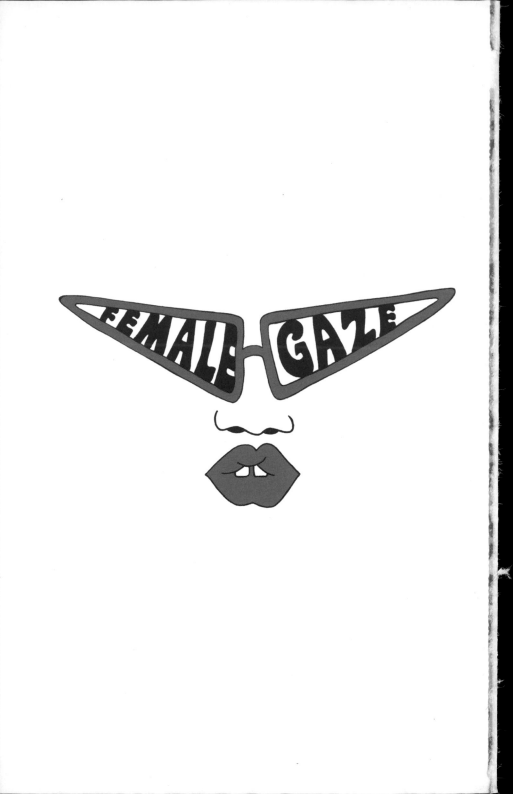

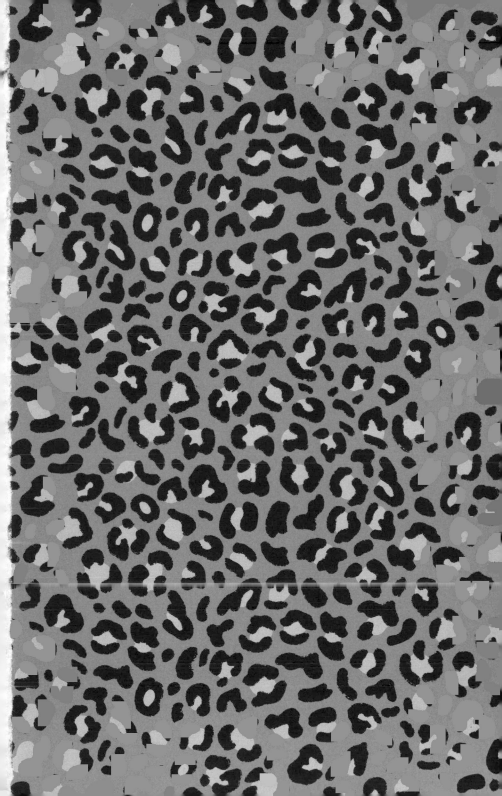

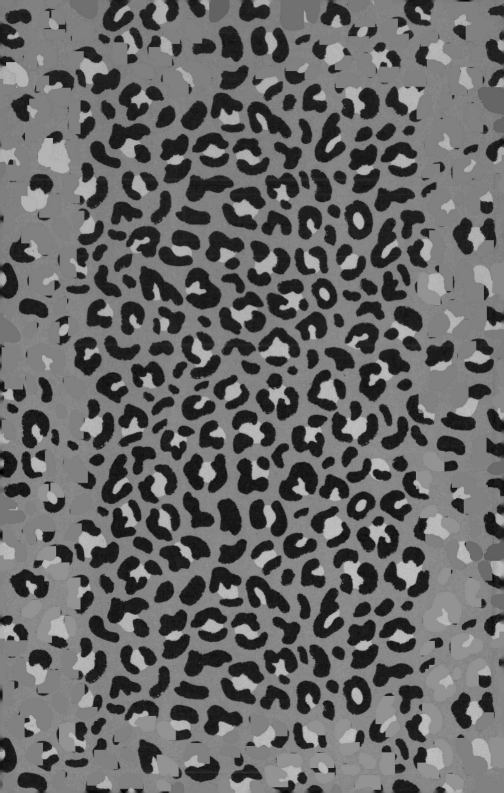